The Mao of Business

The Mao of Business

Guerrilla Trade Techniques for the New China

Peter Levenda

continuum

NEW YORK • LONDON

The Continuum International Publishing Group Inc
80 Maiden Lane, New York, NY 10038

The Continuum International Publishing Group Ltd
The Tower Building, 11 York Road, London SE1 7NX

www.continuumbooks.com

Library of Congress Cataloging-in-Publication Data

Levenda, Peter.
  The Mao of business : guerrilla marketing techniques for the new
China / Peter Levenda.
     p. cm.
  Includes bibliographical references and index.
  ISBN-13: 978-0-8264-2851-6 (hardcover : alk. paper)
  ISBN-10: 0-8264-2851-7 (hardcover : alk. paper)
1. Marketing—China. 2. Negotiation in business—China. 3. Business
etiquette—China. 4. China—Social life and customs. I. Title.
HF5415.12.C5L48 2007
658.800951—dc22

2007026277

Printed in the United States of America

Contents

To Anthony Chang, who brought me to China

and

to Peter Wong, who kept me there

and

to Benson, who never made it back

Foreword

The inspiration for some books seems to come almost by accident, when an author stumbles serendipitously across a new idea or finding in research. At the other end of the spectrum are books that appear to be the natural outgrowth of the author's extensive experience and wisdom, as if the work is a byproduct of their destiny.

The Mao of Business is an ideal example of the latter type of book. It reflects the fact that Peter Levenda spent over twenty years conducting business negotiations in China and other parts of East Asia, where he gained an intimate familiarity with every aspect of the topic.

Known for his previous two books dealing critically with Western esotericism, *Sinister Forces—The Manson Secret: A Grimoire of American Political Witchcraft* and *Unholy Alliance: A History of the Nazi Involvement with the Occult*, Levenda here provides a compelling account of the business world in China. *The Mao of Business* is a must-read at a time when China has been propelled into the role of being a major player on the global economic stage and marketplace.

In the early 1980s, not long after the death of Mao and the ascendancy of Deng precipitated China's move toward capitalism following several decades of Communist isolationism and the effects of the Cultural Revolution,

Levenda helped pioneer what was then virgin territory for international trade. We can only imagine the challenges and struggles that were faced at the time by those trying to penetrate the depths of cross-cultural understanding to facilitate the new enterprise of business transactions. What unavoidable misfires and wrong turns were encountered before they got it right? Levenda emerged from the cocoon of this experience a seasoned and knowledgeable negotiator whose work offers powerful insights and practical wisdom on every page.

In an era when many books are being published that try to relate traditional Chinese notions of the Dao (or Way) or the Art of War to contemporary commerce, Levenda's work stands out for its breakthrough understanding. He convincingly explains that the generation of Chinese businessmen with whom Westerners are now negotiating grew up during a period in which they were not exposed to ancient cosmology or strategy, as these texts were banned or otherwise unavailable. Instead, the Chinese learned their methods and techniques from one little red book that contained the sayings of Chairman Mao, whose comments are based on years of undertaking the Long March and other aspects of ongoing guerrilla warfare.

It is crucial for successful negotiations, Levenda shows the Western reader, to comprehend deeply the implications of Mao's philosophy. Learning well this text and the lessons it contains leads to success, but neglecting or mistaking its intentions results in failure.

Whereas the Regular Army, which is akin to a Fortune 500 company, wages pitched battles with long supply lines and the use of saturation bombing to take cities and important sites, the Guerrilla Army, which is akin to an SME, employs hit-and-run techniques while living off the land and building popular support to take the small towns first. Furthermore, the Regular Army sticks stubbornly to its fixed headquarters and chain of command for the sake of a short-term strategy based on large budgets and intensive marketing campaigns, while the Guerrilla Army flexibly has a moveable and loosely organized headquarters exercising local autonomy for the sake of a long-term strategy of total conversion of the market. Rather than thinking Inside the Box, the guerilla approach boldly asks, "What Box?"

A prime illustration is the third of the nine chapters in the book that depict stratagems derived from Maoist thought, which cites the saying, "Use the villages to encircle the city." According to Levenda's interpretation, applying Mao's tactic of concentrating on the small villages first so that later you can move on to the cities means that if you start with smaller projects it will be easier in the long run to handle big ones. By being a small company you can "move fast, and recover from adversity more quickly, because you have spent a lot less money." Another advantage to starting small is that this places you "closer to the local environment," thus avoiding the pitfall of remaining an irregular (foreigner/outsider) in a land that highly values insider connections (*guanxi*).

Levenda further describes how you need to be patient when doing business in China, because things take time to unfold. When you face problems in the villages, like bad communication, "poor transportation, questionable lodgings, and a lot of time spent on waiting," just remember that the villages will help you get to the cities.

To cite another key example, Levenda's eighth stratagem is based on Mao's saying, "Weapons are an important factor in war, but not the decisive factor; it is people, not things, that are decisive." The significance of this is to learn to be open-minded and ask for advice when you need it, while remembering that the Chinese have been in business for a long time and know what they are doing. When there is a problem you should openly discuss it in order to solve it. One way to steer free from problems within your company is to take a page from Mao's book by treating your employees in an equal way so that there are no preferences.

The Mao of Business also provides practical pointers on lifestyle and behavior, that is, what to do and not do as a foreigner facing strange customs while staying in China, where the local people can be unforgiving in their judgment of a rude or intrusive outsider. Levenda's recommendations include how to comport oneself when eating or during a meeting, and how you should ship your goods, provide proper documentation, and so on.

In conclusion, let me say that Peter Levenda is a gentleman and a scholar in the truest sense of the phrase. It has been a rare privilege for me to know and work with him as a student and friend for the past few years. And it is a special honor to have an opportunity to contribute this piece because it puts me in the same category as Norman Mailer, one of the giants in the history of American letters, who wrote the foreword for another of Mr. Levenda's books.

—Steven Heine, Professor of Religious Studies and History and Director of the Institute for Asian Studies, Florida International University, Miami

Preface
From Tao to Mao

Throw a BlackBerry out of a window in any busy American city and chances are you will hit a China trader . . . who will then pick it up and call everyone on your contact list to see if they want in on the next big Chinese venture. There's an even better chance that *you* are that China trader, and you threw your BlackBerry out the window in sheer frustration at the false promises, extended delays, renegotiated contracts, and all the slippery sales agents you've had to deal with in the past six months, and the increasingly loud and persistent demands of your boss, your shareholders, and your investors that you make a fortune overnight in China.

In *China.*

What are they, *nuts*?

No, but you are. And before you check yourself into rehab, take a deep breath, crack open a Tsingtao, and read on. Things are not as dire as they seem. You *can* be successful in China trade, even if you are working for a small or medium-sized business (SME). I worked as a China sales manager and vice president for SMEs for most of the last twenty-five years, for companies as large as 300 employees grossing $80 million a year to companies as small as three employees grossing $8 million a year, and we were all successful in China. It can be done. It *should* be done (if nothing else, to recoup some of those billions of US dollars sitting comfortably in Chinese banks!). You can do it. I did, and I'm only a kid from the Bronx.

A lot of the books you will read, or have read, on China and Chinese business concepts are based on the ancient Chinese classics. Books like *The Tao of Business* and translations of Sun-Tzu and Lao-Tzu. Books by academics, which have focused on the underlying philosophies that formed the Chinese worldview. They are valuable, in and of themselves, for the introduction they give to American audiences who have little or no exposure to this very old, venerable civilization. After all, the Chinese have been doing business for about 5,000 years; they must know what they are doing.

But these books are usually designed around anecdotes involving Fortune 500 companies, megacorporations like IBM and GM and Coca-Cola. Companies that can afford to stay in for the long haul. Companies that have global brand-name recognition. Companies that have already won half the battle merely by showing up.

You don't have that luxury, do you? I didn't think so. Neither did I. You and me, we have to work for a living. We have to produce. We have to perform miracles on a pathetic budget, no in-house support mechanisms, no brand-name recognition outside our own small industry, and no experienced personnel.

Plus, all those Chinese business tomes on the shelves at your local bookstore generally tend to ignore one important fact: Chinese people raised in the years since the triumph of the Communist revolution in 1949 (the people who are the decision-makers today) did not read the ancient Chinese classics. They did not read Lao-Tzu, did not consult the yarrow stalks of the *I Ching*, and did not bow to their ancestors or memorize Confucius. They could not tell *yin* from *yang*. They had only one spiritual and ethical force in their lives, and the compass of their souls pointed in only one direction: at Chairman Mao Ze Dong. And their "Chinese classic" was Mao's *Little Red Book*.

Mao, not Tao.

When I first started doing China trade in 1984, the Chinese I met had never heard of Lao Tzu (or if they had, they would not admit it). Many of them were young, the same generation as myself, born in the post-war baby boom. They were brought up on "Marxism-Leninism and Mao Ze Dong Thought." There was no religion (the churches and temples had all been closed), and philosophy courses were few and far between. When, on a napkin in a restaurant off Wangfujing, I drew the familiar yin-yang symbol (an unavoidable emblem decorating the bodies of Volkswagen vans in the sixties right next to flower and peace symbol decals), it drew a blank. The *I Ching*? Never heard of it. When I brought out my copy of that revered manual of divination and philosophy it was considered some kind of strange curiosity, like fortune cookies. Mao himself considered Lao-Tzu and Confucius to be embarrassments and representative of a pernicious tendency toward self-interest and individuality at the expense of society and the proletariat.

As it happens, my exposure to Maoism in New York City during the agitated sixties did me more good than my study of ancient Chinese scriptures, for I had brought with me that other pole of Chinese thought: *Quotations from Chairman Mao Tse-Tung*.[1]

A compilation of Mao's sayings, culled from speeches and writings over the years and covering a wide range of issues, this small, prayer-book-sized paperback bound in a Communist-red plastic cover and known popularly as The *Little Red Book* was in every home, in every office, and in the backpack of every soldier of the People's Liberation Army. During the Cultural Revolution, Americans watching the news on television would gaze in horror at the tens of thousands of Chinese men and women wearing nearly identical Mao jackets and caps in

---

1. This was the spelling of the man's name on my English-language copy, printed in Beijing in 1967. Mao Tse-Tung has since been Romanized as Mao Ze Dong, which is how he will be identified in the remainder of this book.

Tian An Men Square waving their copies of the *Book* at the cameras. It is not hyperbole to suggest that Mao's *Book* was the Bible of the Chinese post-war generation.

Containing such pithy and unforgettable utterances as "Political power grows out of the barrel of a gun," the *Book* was also required reading for a generation of American and European (not to mention African and Asian) political activists, revolutionaries, and fellow-travelers. Spanish translations could be found all over Latin America, as indigenous revolutionary groups sought to overthrow right-wing dictatorships in Argentina, Brazil, Chile, Bolivia, and elsewhere. *Sendero Luminoso* ("Shining Path") in Peru, a Maoist guerrilla organization, was heavily influenced by it. So were African revolutionary movements and, today, violent opposition groups in Nepal (among many others). But the *Book* contains more than military strategy and political theory; it also contains comments on everything from education to culture and art, from women and cadres to "Methods of Thinking and Methods of Work." It was believed to be applicable to virtually every situation in which a good Maoist would find him or herself. It represents a complete worldview, especially when taken together with the works of Marx and Lenin and with the larger collections of Mao's writings.

In fact, during the Cultural Revolution, the only wedding gift deemed politically correct was a copy of the *Book* (or a statue of Chairman Mao, waving and smiling benignly); this led to an embarrassment of riches, of course, as the bride and groom would gaze in something akin to disbelieving awe at a table piled high with the wedding gifts: stacks of the *Little Red Book* and armies of Chairman Mao statues!

Thus, the thrust of my argument and the basis for the approach taken in this book: one cannot hope to understand the Chinese people of today—in particular the middle-aged Chinese who are in charge of the Party and in charge of the economy—unless one also understands the theories and philosophy of Chairman Mao. The effect of

Maoism on China has been deep and profound. Although China has come to terms with the truth of his regime—the brutality, the terror, the mass murder, and the sheer stupidity—he is still the Father of the Country, the man who gave China its independence from foreign powers, and its freedom from the greedy and unscrupulous upper classes. The emotional response of the average Chinese person to Mao is one of conflict and paradox. They are embarrassed by him . . . and they love him. They despise the devastating effects of some of his more outlandish programs—the Great Leap Forward, the Cultural Revolution, to name but two—and they cherish the fact that, because of Mao, China is now a superpower and an economic juggernaut. The visionary reforms of Deng Xiao Ping ("To be rich is glorious!") never would have been put into place had it not been for a free China, an organized China, a China that had found its own identity after hundreds of years of domestic corruption and foreign intervention and colonialism: a China that would not have existed had it not been for Chairman Mao.

Of course, Mao might be rolling over in his tomb to see what has happened to China since his death in 1976: the neon-lit thoroughfares, the futuristic skyscrapers, and the young people dressed in Western fashions, shouting over cell phones and surfing the Net, dancing in discos until all hours ("To get drunk is glorious!"): capitalism run amok.

And then again, he might be proud. Because for Mao— as for the Chinese themselves—Communism and Marxism-Leninism was one thing, but to see a strong and proud China, able to defend itself, able to make its voice heard on the world stage, is quite another.

In this book we will examine this mentality and try to find a way of using this much-neglected aspect of Chinese philosophy—Maoism—to develop strategies for doing business in China and, by extension, doing business anywhere. For Mao was first and foremost a guerrilla leader, a man who led impossibly outnumbered and outfinanced forces against larger, better-equipped, and better-trained

Introduction
Notes from an Old China Hand

Anyone who thinks international business is glamorous—the stuff of secret agents and exotic Asian assassins, perfectly mixed martinis and soft leather chairs in exclusive clubs—has never spent a four-hour layover in Narita Airport after flying for twelve, sitting in small seats with backrests that only come up to your shoulder blades, stomach growling for any morsel of food while the concession stands remain suspiciously closed. It's almost enough to pray for a masked ninja with an attitude and a samurai sword, or an exotic assassin to take you out of your misery. "What's the yen doing today?" Anthony Chang would ask me as we waited for our connecting flight to Beijing.

"It's still at 107," I would reply. "It hasn't moved much."

Anthony would start calculating cost and sales, moving his right index finger in the air as if he was moving the beads of an imaginary abacus. "And the Swedish krone?"

"We'll take a bath on that unless we can convince the Chinese to pay in krone instead of dollars . . ." We had sold high-voltage power cable to the city of Xian from our supplier, Ericsson Cables of Sweden. But the exchange rates were killing us as the dollar dropped in value against the Japanese yen and the Swedish krone.

It was 1986, and I was on my first trip to China in what would become a major career move and lifelong obsession. That trip would cause me to question many preconceived notions, not only about doing business in China but also about China itself: its language, its history, its culture, its political and economic structure, and its people. What I learned is summarized in the pages that follow. Some of what I say will be controversial, but it is my intention that all of it will be educational and valuable to those of you who are committed to investing your time, your money, your career, and your energy in this most dynamic and most addictive of foreign markets. One of the more controversial elements of this approach is the value and emphasis I place on the writings of New China's most famous—and infamous—personality: Chairman Mao Ze Dong. Alone among the spate of business books about China and applying Chinese philosophy—Lao Tzu, Sun Tzu, Confucius, and others—to business, this book takes the pragmatic and realistic stand that one cannot hope to understand China without understanding something of Mao's philosophy and the role that Maoism has played in creating modern China. It also emphasizes the fact that today's decision-makers in China—your customers—were brought up in the Maoist era. They exulted over the success of the Revolution, they suffered under the excesses of the Great Leap Forward and the Cultural Revolution, they breathed a sigh of relief when Deng Xiaoping took over after Mao's death in 1976. Some were on the winning side—the cadres, the government ministers, the army officers, the Red Guard—and others were on the losing side: the intellectuals, the factory directors, the engineers. You will meet them all in China, and it is important to understand the ideas that made such an impact on their lives and which, for better or worse, influence them to this day.

I first began studying Mandarin in 1971. My initial purpose was the translation of ancient Chinese alchemical texts that had not yet appeared in English. I thought that I could demonstrate that European alchemy had its

origins in the more biologically oriented alchemical practices of Chinese Daoism and Indian Tantricism, transmit-
ted perhaps along the Silk Route. (Why would I want to
do that? What can I say? I was a strange youth and it was
the sixties.)

Then, about a year after my study began, I wound up
in the hospital with a collapsed lung. It was Thanksgiving
week. There were no thoracic surgeons available in the
entire New York City area, except for a tall Chinese doctor
from the "mainland" who was connected with the United
Nations in some capacity. I found myself being operated
on in Beekman Downtown Hospital, which is located near
Chinatown, and which had at the time a largely Chinese
staff with signs in both English and Chinese characters. It
was an oddly appropriate place to wind up. I was able to
continue my studies in Mandarin from my hospital bed, as
Chinese nurses and medtechs drew blood, checked vitals,
and took x-rays.

The problem was that Mandarin was not a popular
language to study in New York City in the early seventies. There was one course at NYU, but for the most part
Cantonese was the "dialect" most widely spoken in
Chinatown, along with Hokkien and a few other southern "dialects." The Chinese characters used in the newspapers and signage were the traditional ones, not the
simplified characters I had been studying from the text-
books that had been published in Beijing. Once I was dis-
charged from the hospital, I learned that the school where
I had been taking intensive, deep-immersion courses in
Mandarin—Educational Solutions—no longer offered the
subject due to a lack of interested students.

I was back where I started. Fortunately, there was
another option. On West Fourth Street in Manhattan at the
time was a popular Asian supplies store called China
Center. It was run by a Chinese family who had lived in
the People's Republic of China (PRC) but who had eventually managed to make it to New York. Their store was an
amazing collection of artifacts from China—including
teas, herbal medicines, Mao jackets and pins, and books in

Chinese. I made friends with the family, bought a Mao jacket and the *Little Red Book*, and they eventually agreed to teach me Mandarin. The tutor in this case was a charming young woman by the name of Gigi Yang. Slowly, using the Beijing workbooks, I began to learn the tones and the vocabulary of Mandarin Chinese.

Is there such a thing as the "Chinese" language? If by "Chinese" we mean any language that is spoken in the political entity we know as the People's Republic of China, then we are left with the unpleasant task of including everything from Tibetan to Uighur under the rubric "Chinese." If, instead, we choose to include only those languages that use the Chinese character set as "Chinese," then we are forced to include some ancient Japanese and Korean works as well, works written before Japan and Korea had developed their own writing systems.

What, then, is "Chinese"? To answer that question is to confront what it means to be a citizen of modern China, or what the optimists call "New China." It is to understand the legacy of Chairman Mao, and to understand the role of the emperor of China since ancient times and down to the modern Politburo and Central Committee, for China faces (and has always faced) a situation of governance—and hence of economics—that is becoming increasingly common throughout the world: the management of a multilingual, multiethnic society.

In the meantime, however, I was also concerned with making a living and worked for six years for the Bendix Corporation in midtown Manhattan and, after that, for Bank Hapoalim at Rockefeller Center. My international horizons were expanding in every direction, and after four years at the Israeli bank I found myself at a tiny import-export firm in lower Manhattan—in the shadow of the World Trade Center—and preparing to go to China to make my employer's fortune. By that time, China Center had disappeared—it closed mysteriously one month when I was away—and with it my only chance of learning

Mandarin in my spare time. Yet, I had not realized just how much I had managed to learn; in the summer of 1986, I found myself sitting in Narita Airport in Japan waiting for my connecting flight to Hong Kong.

My mentor and travel partner was Anthony Chang, a man born in Yentai in Shandong Province and whose father had been an international businessman. Anthony Chang went to school in the United States after Mao's revolution made China an uncomfortable place for capitalists, even as the rest of his family remained behind in China and eventually rose to secure positions in government and medicine, weathering all the political storms that followed the success of the revolution. As for Anthony, he eventually wound up doing business in Asia and made a successful living during the Vietnam War selling automotive spare parts and other commodities. What I know today about China trade is largely the legacy of Anthony Chang and of another man, Peter Wong, who will also figure prominently in this story.

My first day in China itself was an eye-opener. It was summer, and Beijing was wreathed in smog and haze. In the distance, I could see the formidable façade of the Forbidden City with Mao's portrait hung over the entrance, a little like the Wizard in *The Wizard of Oz* . . . but we were not going there. Instead, we were eating a hurried lunch in an ancient restaurant with several people who had come to meet us and escort us by van several hours to the south of the capitol, to the factory town of Baoding. The conversation was quiet, the slowly moving fans above our heads serving to push the air around but not much else, and the food . . . the food was unlike anything I had ever eaten in any Chinese restaurant in the United States. Things were jellied, pickled, and served lukewarm. There was sea cucumber, a noxious worm of a dish that looked like sliced brown gelatin and tasted like congealed fat. (Oddly enough, it was a dish I learned to appreciate and wound up ordering on my own, back in the States.) There were some small, unidentifiable birds, deep-fried with heads and beaks intact. Warm soft drinks. A steamed fish that looked happy to have lost its life, relieved at the end of its suffering in the cruelty of a hot Beijing summer's day.

All around me, everyone was wearing a Mao jacket. Some people wore socks, most did not or, if they did, they were nylon, which must have been murder in that weather. Trousers were old, torn, occasionally a little soiled, and worn by men and women alike ... those women who were not wearing long skirts below the knee and nylon stockings that only came up below the knee. There was a cacophony of sound on the street outside the restaurant, which only made the heat seem hotter: bicycle bells ringing madly, people shouting, a loudspeaker blaring some kind of scratchy music interspersed with slogans and speeches, truck drivers grinding gears, and above it all children laughing.

Lunch was over in under two hours. We got up from the table and went downstairs to the waiting van. Our suitcases were already in it, and we jumped inside for the insane drive down to Baoding, a drive during which Anthony and I—as foreigners—were not allowed to get out for any reason, because the area we were driving through was considered "closed" to foreigners.

There were masses of people, vehicles, and animals on the road all the way to Baoding. These were people who looked as if they had spent their lives living rough; weathered people, people whose daily struggle to survive was etched into their faces with a heavy hand. Our driver depended more on his horn than his brakes as we made good time, dividing the Red sea before us as people simply walked in front of our van, oblivious to our existence, getting out of the way only at the very last moment when I was certain we were going to run over bicycles, children, donkeys, cows, old men carrying huge burdens, young women with aged features and rough, reddened hands, and the occasional policeman or military man. (I couldn't tell the difference in those days between the greenish uniforms of the Army and the greenish uniforms of the police.) Occasionally we were stopped and had to show our passports, but in general there was nothing to impede our way and we arrived in Baoding in time for dinner. With the mayor of the city.

It was at that moment that I learned the first important lesson of my career in China trade. You'll read about it in all the books, articles, and documentaries. It's called *guanxi* and it's a Mandarin word meaning "connections." Nothing gets done in China without *guanxi*, and Anthony Chang was rolling in it.

In the days, weeks, and months that followed, I learned the basic lessons that form the core of this book. With the passage of decades, those lessons have been revisited, honed, and expanded, but they nonetheless remain the same in essence. My knowledge of the *Little Red Book* and of Mao's revolution in general helped me a great deal, not only in understanding the mentality of the people I was dealing with but also in overcoming suspicion and hostility. After all, I was a foreigner who had read Mao. Had I been the foreigner who had read Sun Tzu or Lao Tzu, it would not have made much difference; the fact that I could quote Mao meant that I was somehow an admirer, someone who understood Mao's relevance and importance, someone who did not see Mao as a threat and, hence, did not see China as a menace. I was someone they could deal with, someone with whom they shared at least one common fascination:

The thought of Chairman Mao Ze Dong.

Chapter 1
The First Stratagem

Guerrilla warfare ... is a weapon that a nation inferior in arms and military equipment may employ against a more powerful aggressor nation.
—Chairman Mao

As someone responsible for sales and marketing in China, you face several opponents: the foreign companies that have been in the market already and have seized large chunks of the available market, local Chinese companies and manufacturers, and the Chinese environment itself, which does not support normative Western business practices. For the sake of argument, let us assume that you are working within a tight budget and with an impossible sales target. The vast nation called China—or the People's Republic of China (PRC) and never "Red China" or "mainland China"—looms before you, seemingly monolithic and certainly imposing. What do you do?

To begin, you must take stock of who you are and what tools you have available. You are a guerrilla warrior, in the mold of Mao and his revolutionary forces. You cannot fight a pitched battle against General Motors, or

IBM, or Coca-Cola, or whoever your major competitor happens to be. The tactic you must employ is hit-and-run; the overall strategy is to weaken your opponent's defenses from the inside.

Think Hannibal. Think Major Mosby. Think Viet Cong.

Your tools—your "arms and military equipment" as the Chairman would say—are your intelligence, your pragmatism, and your keen sense of strategy and tactics. Ambition is one thing, but you must keep focused on smaller, attainable goals in the first few months or the first year of China trade, for those smaller victories will finance your later campaigns. But before we get into details, let's make sure we understand the big picture first.

When we talk of Chairman Mao, we have to differentiate between the Good Mao and the Bad Mao. Good Mao was the Mao of the Revolution, a man who represented courage, resourcefulness, and clear and pragmatic thinking: thinking "outside the box."

Bad Mao was the Mao of the Great Leap Forward, and the Cultural Revolution; a man who represented an overwhelming ego, combined with stupid mistakes, brutality, paranoia, and the fatal weakness of believing in one's own propaganda. A man who became the epitome of what Marx called the "Cult of Personality."

Obviously, we want to emulate the Good Mao, the Mao who was the Father of his Country, the man who made China proud. How do we do that and avoid the excesses of the Bad Mao?

For a start, let's compare Mao's China to Stalin's Russia, both Communist countries, one of which exists no longer.

The Soviet Union under Stalin and under most of its later leaders was concerned with spreading Communism throughout the world: an ambitious sales campaign that required a massive investment in international markets. The USSR extended its reach into

Eastern Europe, the "captive" nations and the "satellite" nations. It also embroiled itself in conflicts from Africa to Asia to Latin America. We can say that the Soviet Union tried to be in too many markets, too soon—a fact that weakened them at home. The eventual fall of the Soviet Union indicated to the world that it was Russia, not the United States, that was a "paper tiger."

China, on the other hand, withdrew from the world in the years following the success of their Revolution. With the exception of the "police action" in Korea, Chinese military forces were used to consolidate its own position internally in its many provinces, including the hotly contested Tibet.[1] Chinese military build-up was concentrated on its borders with Russia and India, and to some extent Southeast Asia (especially Vietnam, which was receiving Soviet support during its war with the United States). Although China was happy to export its brand of "Marxism-Leninism and Mao Ze Dong Thought" wherever it could, it did not have the resources to engage in the kind of military adventurism so typical of the Soviet Union. When it did go "overseas"—Korea, Tibet, etc.—it was restricted to Asia and to "markets" it already knew well. It did not invest heavily in foreign campaigns; instead, its focus was on strengthening its home base.

There is a lesson here for all of us.

When it comes to investing—time, money, personnel—in China trade, your first duty is to make certain that your company can handle the weight. If you try to do business in China while your domestic business is

---

1. Is Tibet really part of China? Well, it is now. The historical evidence China provides to justify its invasion and the excesses of the Cultural Revolution that was responsible for the destruction of many of Tibet's religious and cultural treasures is flimsy, to say the least. Tibet is a subject best not brought up during your sales mission to China; but that doesn't mean you have to swallow the Party line.

shaky, or when you are looking at mounting debt, investing in China trade could sink you. This is not a venture for the faint of heart, the tyro, or the dilettante. Further, do not attempt to penetrate too many markets at once. Give each a little room to breathe and to grow. China will demand a great deal of you and your company as the business starts to heat up; it will tend to drain resources from other areas until it turns profitable. If those other areas are mature sectors of your business, then you should be able to handle the cash flow. If, however, these other areas are also new markets for you—Japan, say, or Korea—then all of them may suffer. Don't make the Soviet mistake of extending yourself into too many markets at once. Remember that the United States (and its allies) outspent the Soviet Union, essentially bankrupting the Russian state rather than invading it. International business, and your wealthier competitors, can do the same to you if you are not careful.

Which brings us to expenses.

Your costs at first will be largely travel-related. It isn't cheap to fly to China and remain there for any length of time (although ground arrangements are usually less expensive than, say, Europe), and you can't expect to win a contract on the first trip out. What you can do, however, is maximize every moment you are in-country by using a variety of resources that are cost-effective. This means looking at your approach from the point of view of a guerrilla warrior.

Guerrilla Warfare: Mao versus Tao

What happens when the dao prevails in the state? It becomes a matter of shame for one to be poor and base.

—Chairman Mao

In the first place, Mao utilized a form of warfare—guerrilla warfare—that was based on living off the land and using local support systems to keep his army fed and to keep valuable intelligence coming his way while at the same time building popular support among the civilian populations in the areas he came across. You will need to do much the same at this stage. In fact, you can begin developing local contacts in the marketplace long before you catch your first flight to Beijing. They may not be trustworthy; they may be unreliable or fickle. But they are vitally necessary at this preliminary stage and will probably remain that way for the rest of your career in China trade. You simply have to learn how to take advantage of their positive attributes and protect yourself against their negative ones. We will examine the role of the sales agent later on in this study; for now, though, let us look at the advantages to conducting a Mao-style guerrilla sales campaign.

How does guerrilla strategy help you in becoming successful in China? Well, guerrilla warfare created the modern China. It's a form of conflict that works very well in the kind of environment China offers: a huge landmass, ethnically diverse populations, extended and weakened communication and transportation lines, widespread poverty, and a natural suspicion of events taking place in the capitol. Add to this the growing influence of foreign culture and economic ideas, as well as the newly created license and encouragement for the average Chinese person to make a profit (something that did not exist in the first decade of my business experience in China), and you have a volatile marketplace, vulnerable to the kind of hit-and-run creative marketing that is essential for SMEs desiring to succeed there.

Let's look at how Maoist guerrilla tactics can be used against the type of "pitched battle" mentality normally employed by Fortune 500 companies in China. (These same techniques can also be used in other markets, even your own.)

Regular Army (Fortune 500)	Guerrilla Army (SME)
Pitched battles	Hit and run
Long supply lines	Live off the land
Take cities and important sites	Take the small towns
Saturation bombing	Build popular support
Fixed headquarters	Moveable headquarters
Fixed chain of command	Local autonomy, loosely organized
Short-term strategy based on large budgets	Long-term strategy of total and intensive marketing campaigns conversion of the market
Thinking inside the box	What box?

Let's look at them one at a time.

Hit and Run

> **The enemy advances, we retreat; the enemy camps, we harass; the enemy tires, we attack; the enemy retreats, we pursue.**
>
> **—Chairman Mao**

If you had to choose one word to characterize the guerrilla approach it would probably have to be "flexibility." Most large organizations have one important disadvantage: they can't turn on a dime. They can't make quick decisions and react swiftly to market conditions. They have meetings, and more meetings, and worry about the effect on their shareholders. They perform studies, and hire consultants, and spend a fortune in fact-finding trips (which become little more than junkets). A small organization, on the other hand, can make a decision and implement changes quickly and generally decrease reaction time. It's hard to make a Fortune 500 company move; there are too many internal departments and red tape. That is your chief advantage, and you should respect it. It will win you contracts before the larger, more famous company even knows they are up for negotiation.

Live Off the Land

> **Whoever wants to know a thing has no way of doing so except by coming into contact with it, that is, by living (practicing) in its environment. . . . All genuine knowledge originates in direct experience.**
> **—Chairman Mao**

There are two ways to interpret this suggestion. The first may be a little counterintuitive.

It would be a mistake to become actively involved in China trade while at the same time keeping China itself at a distance. You have to get to know the country, and not only from books (like this one) but from direct experience. You have to walk the streets, look at the buildings and the infrastructure, eat in the restaurants, and get a feel for the terrain. There is a lot of information encoded in every city's design and culture, some of which may help you at a crucial time.

For instance, during one very important sales negotiation, I had the engineers who were with me visit the proposed site in advance of the meeting with the clients. This was for a telecommunications wiring project that would become very high profile, and thus very important to my company. I had the engineers walk the site, take in the side streets, look at everything. I had nothing particular in mind, but I wanted them to know the area perfectly and to get an idea of how the proposed construction project meshed with the neighborhood.

When the time came for the technical aspect of the sales negotiation—which, of course, always precedes the actual sales negotiation itself—my team was much better prepared than our competitors who represented large, very well-known American companies that had not bothered to get their shoes dirty in the mud of the site itself but that relied upon blueprints provided by the customer to tell the whole story. In China, such preliminary blueprints are not to be relied upon (something I knew from bitter experience). Instead, my engineers had noted all the ways in which the actual site differed from the blueprints, and were therefore able to offer suggestions as to how the construction and installation project could proceed in a more cost-effective and technically viable manner. Our competitors were left flat-footed and failed the technical presentation. (They came back at us later in an attempt to steal the project from us, but that is another story to be told later on.)

When we speak of "living off the land," of course, we mean more than just paying attention. We also mean living cheaply and close to the bone. This means taking advantage of local hotels and restaurants and hiring local personnel when it comes time to open an office in China, and using local advertising companies and advertising designers. Traveling in China can be inexpensive if you travel like a local. That means avoiding the big, foreign-owned hotels—the Marriotts and the Hiltons—and sticking with the three-star and even two-star hotels that cater to a largely Chinese clientele. Any good guidebook will identify the reputable ones for you, and especially the ones where the staff speaks some English and the restaurant has menus in English as well as Chinese. When you have to impress a customer, take them to a fancy restaurant (even one in a Marriott or a Hilton); but when you're on your own, you can afford to be more frugal. In fact, my good friend and old China hand Peter Wong and I used to frequent a hotel in Shanghai that was located directly behind the Shanghai

Hilton. The rooms in the Chinese hotel cost a lot less, but we only had to walk down a short path from our hotel to the rear entrance of the Hilton in order to use the latter's sumptuous facilities, from its restaurants to its bar, its travel agent, and its office facilities (such as fax machines and photocopiers). You won't always find a sweet arrangement like that, but it pays to keep your eyes open to take advantage of any such opportunities as they come along.

You will also want to be sure to have any advertising you are using printed and designed in China itself. This is for several reasons. In the first place, China is very inexpensive when it comes to printing (many American and European publishing companies have already discovered this important fact). In the second place, shipping printed material from your home office to China is expensive and sometimes unreliable. In the third place, and perhaps most important of all, the type of printed Chinese that is common abroad is not normative in China itself. China uses a modernized system of writing and printing Chinese characters which the rest of the Chinese-speaking world has been slow to adopt—for political as well as cultural reasons. Any Chinese client you have will notice the difference right away. Further, Chinese slang proceeds in a different direction in China from that in other places, such as Taiwan or the Chinatowns of New York or San Francisco. You may find yourself printing what you think are clever advertising slogans but which actually mean something quite different in China. As an example, I once had to cancel an advertising campaign my company was running based on cartoons of some cute kittens, because the word for "cat" in Mandarin is the same as that for the Chairman: *mao*. In China, the picture of a cat is sometimes used by critics as a coded means of referring to Chairman Mao.

Living off the land will repay itself not only in terms of expenses, but as you can see also in terms of knowing your business environment. Getting your shoes and your hands dirty is one way of understanding the world in which your customers live, and it will not only save you money in the long run, it will also earn you money.

Take the Small Towns

Attack dispersed, isolated enemy forces first; attack concentrated, strong enemy forces later. Take small and medium cities and extensive rural areas first; take big cities later.

—Chairman Mao

Some companies get positively dizzy and fall into rapturous swoons when they think of China trade. All those people. All those customers. They are dazzled by photographs and documentaries about Beijing and Shanghai and Hong Kong: cities that seem like modern marvels, flashy, neon-lit *Blade Runner* terrain but minus the deranged anthropoid killers. They want to make a killing in China themselves, and they have visions of winning large projects in the big cities.

Mao understood that the big cities had to come last. First, he had to win the hearts and minds of the people in the countryside, or else he couldn't hold onto the big cities. He had to encircle the cities by conquering the small towns. When he had popular support in the countryside, the larger cities would fall.

Your approach to China trade should incorporate this strategy. There is a lot of potential wealth waiting in the countryside, particularly as your foreign competitors will tend to avoid the small towns in favor of the comfort of doing business in the more modern industrial and commercial centers.

My first sales in China were in the relatively small (at that time) town of Baoding, in Hebei Province, which boasted a number of factories, including those for the manufacture of rayon (the second largest such plant in China), for roofing materials, and for rubber hose and molding. The company I worked for—a small import-export firm in Lower Manhattan—did most of its China trade in the years 1984–1988 in Baoding, doing millions of dollars there each year. With the reputation we built in Baoding we were able to demonstrate to clients in other cities that we were reliable, competent, and knowledge-able: not a small thing in China. Word spread. One morning, after one such business expedition to Baoding had been successfully completed, I was awakened by a knock at the door at seven in the morning in my room at the Beijing Hotel only to find a delegation numbering eight people waiting outside, eager to discuss another business proposal. I had no idea who they were, or indeed that anyone at all was scheduled to show up that day. They had simply heard that I was back in town and wanted to talk business. They represented one of the energy ministries, based in Beijing itself. In other words, we had successfully used the small towns to circle the big city.

Later on, when I was working for a larger firm, we employed the same strategy. Many of our American competitors focused on the large, high-profile projects in Beijing and Shanghai. We knew that there was a lot of business in the cities and towns outside of the major metropolitan areas, and especially (at the time) in Szechuan Province and in Guangdong (Canton) Province. By picking up a few relatively low-profit jobs in these areas, we were able to point to our track record when it came to seeking the bigger jobs in Beijing and Shanghai. These smaller projects also helped us to finance our presence in China, and to prove to our CEO and CFO that we could be successful in that country; that meant that we had more support from the head office, which was only too happy to boast to their friends and investors that they were "in China." We will discuss this strategy in greater depth a little later on.

Build Popular Support

> **Take the ideas of the masses and concentrate them, then go to the masses, persevere in the ideas and carry them through, so as to form correct ideas of leadership. . . .**
>
> **—Chairman Mao**

The Fortune 500 firms often focus on the chief executives of the clients they are wooing. They wine and dine the factory directors, the general managers, and others in that rarified atmosphere while ignoring the personnel lower down in the hierarchy. Mao's approach to guerrilla warfare can teach us something about that, too.

Before Mao, guerrilla warriors would not attempt to build rapport with the people in the towns and villages they passed through. In fact, they might often steal food and other supplies in the dead of night and slip away into the darkness to harass the enemy. They would view civilians with suspicion, or as people who were simply in the way. Mao understood that civilians had a vital role to play in the revolution. If he could put his philosophy before the peasantry and make his case for armed resistance then he could count on their willing and enthusiastic support in a variety of ways, from providing much-needed intelligence to serving as supply centers, stockpiling food and medicine and other materials needed to keep the revolution going. Mao included the peasants in his plans, made them part of the solution. His opponents saw the civilian, peasant population as something to be browbeaten, raped, and robbed at the point of a sword. Mao's way worked better. It was a perfect *sales* campaign, not just a military campaign.

When I first became involved in China trade, I was impressed by how successful the Japanese were. They were China's enemy from the days of Manchu-Guo and the invasions of the Second World War. They had raped and pillaged throughout the country (as, indeed, they had in much of Asia). There were Chinese alive in the 1980s (and today) who hated the Japanese with a proud passion. Yet, here they were, in their identical black suits and leather briefcases, soaking up all the trade that China had to offer. How were they doing that, I wondered? How did they manage to overcome a generation of bad feelings, distrust, and sheer hostility to become China's largest trading partner (and my chief competitor)?

In the first place, of course, they had a head start. Although the United States only recognized China in the seventies (they had thrown their support behind Chiang Kai-Shek's Republic of China, based in Taiwan), the Japanese lost no time in recognizing the People's Republic of China and had been involved in trade with China longer than the US. China desperately needed high-technology items and equipment for light and heavy manufacturing, and they had nowhere else to go (except Russia and the countries of the Eastern bloc with their inferior products and unreliable supply chains). So, as pragmatic as they are, the Chinese leaders had to swallow their bad feelings and deal with Japan.

For their part, the Japanese understood very well how to approach their Chinese customers. First, they always had at least one member of their delegation who spoke fluent Mandarin. Toward the end of the eighties, most members of the Japanese delegations I ran across spoke Mandarin.

In the second place, they were willing to take their time to win the market. They undersold most everyone else— including European and other trading partners—and were willing to take losses today to ensure market share tomorrow. (At times, they offset their losses by selling less-than-top-quality merchandise or by selling a piece of equipment cheaply, but the spare parts very dear.)

Finally, one of their most brilliant maneuvers was in their approach to gift-giving.

They would always bring with them a warehouse full of Japanese-made presents that they would distribute among all the customer's workers they came across. For the lowliest worker—an office clerk, perhaps, or the person who brought tea—they would give a beautifully made pen. Further up the hierarchy, a radio or a cassette player. Further still, a small television set. And so on. To the chief executives and directors, gifts would be more opulent: Mont Blanc pens, for instance, or bottles of expensive Scotch, genuine leather accessories, or—in at least one case—an automobile.

The important thing to learn, for me, was the fact that they made sure to cover everyone. They knew that a project could succeed or fail due to the cooperation, or lack of it, of even the smallest link in the chain of command. They built popular support and reinforced their image by showering everyone in sight with gifts. Gifts, mind you, not "bribes." As one of my dearest associates from those days in China used to tell me, "A smile and good manners will do you very well in China; a smile, good manners, and a small gift, even more!"

Today, this tactic is "even more" to be observed. Since the iron rice bowl is now broken, and the average Chinese must hustle to make a living and earn enough to buy the important things in life—a refrigerator, an air-conditioner, a washing machine, even one day a car—there is a lot of movement in the employment sector. The secretary you meet today at one company may become the buyer for another company in six months, and usually within the same industry. That means you will run into her later, in a more influential capacity. The employment situation in China is one of constant churn; it is important to remain on friendly terms with everyone you meet, even those working for your competitors. One day, they may come to you looking for a job . . . and bringing their Rolodex (or their BlackBerry) with them!

Moveable Headquarters

Oppose fixed battle lines and positional warfare, and favor fluid battle lines and mobile warfare.
—Chairman Mao

There is nothing worse that you can do in China than sit in your office and wait for business to come to you. In fact, there is nothing worse you can do than sit in any one place for any length of time. Business in China moves across the whole board, from Beijing to Baoding, from Hohhot to Urumqi, from Xian to Yunnan. Your headquarters is wherever you happen to be. You will live out of a briefcase and a suitcase. There is absolutely nothing greater you can do than meet your clients face-to-face, especially in a country that places such a high value on personal relationships.

The Chinese have been burned many times before. They have suffered from colonialism and imperialism. You don't have to be a left-leaning liberal to understand that the basic events of Chinese history over the past two hundred years or more have been centered around the involvement of European and Japanese forces in their business, from the Opium Wars of the eighteenth century to the Japanese invasion of the twentieth century. Shanghai was carved up into foreign "concessions," which operated autonomously in China, completely independent from Chinese government regulations, police, or laws. Hong Kong was a British colony; Macau was Portuguese. And Japan invaded China with an eye to making the whole country a Japanese colony.

Thus, the Chinese have a right to be suspicious of foreigners and their intentions.

So your work is cut out for you when it comes to building relations. Making one good friend in China is fine; making a few hundred is even better. The Chinese do not understand loyalty to a company; to the Chinese, a company is not a real person (Imagine that!). A company cannot be trusted, or relied upon. A company is only as good as the people who compose it. If your client trusts you, he or she will trust you no matter what company you eventually work for. You will take that relationship with you wherever you go in the future. But they have to know you first, and trust you. That means eating with you, drinking with you, talking about nonbusiness-related topics with you, and even singing karaoke with you. They want to see you with your guard down; they believe in the old adage, *in vino veritas*.

They are not going to get this kind of access to your true nature, your real self, while you are sitting in your hotel room or your newly rented office space in Beijing or Shanghai. They want to see you on their turf, in their town, eating their local food and ogling their local women, getting drunk on their local brew.

Also, it is best for you to travel to the customer's headquarters and factories because that is the only way you are going to see the reality of any given situation. As mentioned above, you can obtain one set of impressions from a client's printed material and formal presentations . . . and an entirely different (and more accurate) one from a personal visit to their offices and factories. In addition, the Chinese will respect you more the more you actually travel to see them. That means you should attend seminars and conferences in your industry no matter where in China they may be held. You can use the opportunity to meet more people, network across a broad spectrum of contacts, and advance your own cause by talking up your company and its products.

My personal experience has shown that being the one to conduct the seminar and conference is also extremely valuable in making contacts and showcasing your company. The cost is not as great as you might imagine—especially in the smaller, more remote locations—and attendance can usually be counted upon to be substantial. Throw in lunch, and you're almost guaranteed a full house for whatever it is you want to sell or discuss.

Keep the headquarters moving; be flexible in your own schedule and location as much as possible. It's an old saw, but a good one: go to the business, and the business will come to you.

Local Autonomy, Loosely Organized

Oppose an absolutely centralized command, and favor a relatively centralized command.
—Chairman Mao

Later, as you build your business, you will have staff members in various places in China. We may be talking about only a single person—a sales engineer or sales rep—in another city, or we may be talking about offices local to a given province or region, staffed by any number of personnel. Whatever the arrangement may be, you will be faced with a critical decision to make and one that has plagued many a China trader before you: to what extent do you trust another person, particularly a local national, to run your business?

Trust is a two-way street. Just as you have to take the time to allow your clients to know you and trust you, so you have to take the time to know and trust your own people. The hardest thing for an entrepreneur to do is to let go, and every China trader is an entrepreneur no matter what company he or she works for, or how big it is. Once in China, you will find that you are largely on your own. You can't be everywhere at once, so you will be forced to trust others to handle some aspects of the business for you.

Some companies have "solved" this problem by running a tight ship: a rigid chain of command and a corporate policy book that would choke a panda. They assume that such a no-nonsense approach will solve the problem of trust: make sure there is no room to maneuver, and your employees will have no opportunity to slack off or sell you out.

In response to that, let me quote an adage that does not come from Chairman Mao but from my old mentor, Anthony Chang: "A Chinese businessman keeps three sets of books: one for the government, one for his partner, and one for himself." No amount of red tape, bureaucratic regulations, or corporate policy memos will stand in the way of a sharp Chinese businessperson doing what comes naturally: making a profit for himself or herself. And it is the sharp Chinese businessperson you want working for you and with you. So . . . how to solve this problem?

In the first place, it isn't a problem. You control the purse strings. All your local sales engineer or sales rep can really do is try to cut a deal on the side with your client or even with your competitor. If your rep cuts a side deal with your client, so what? It may seem shady or unethical by Western standards, but what harm has it really done to you and your business? In fact, by using his position with you to advance his own financial well-being he is more likely to continue working for you and winning projects for you. If he cuts a deal with your competitor, however, by giving him proprietary information or telling him your pricing strategy, etc., then he is damaging you and you have no choice but to fire him . . . well, unless by doing that he has lulled your opponent into a false sense of security, leading him into a trap at a crucial stage of negotiation! Naturally, this latter scenario is rare, but it has happened; the problem with it is your rep is pursuing a dangerous strategy you know nothing about, and that is never very good.

We will examine the role of the sales rep, sales engineer, and other tricky Chinese personnel issues a little later on in this book. For now, the message I want to leave with you is simple: your local personnel will always have, and exercise, a certain degree of autonomy whether you are aware of it or not! It is best to allow that degree of flexibility because they know their environment a lot better than you do, and can make decisions on the ground that will improve your position immeasurably. I know that means trusting people you don't really know, and business people hate that. Entrepreneurs hate it even more. But nothing is written in stone, and you can always take steps to mitigate the effects of such autonomy without sacrificing your business. The alternative is to micromanage, and that is difficult enough in your own country with people whose culture and values you share; try doing that ten thousand miles away, in a country whose language does not have a word for "no" . . . and none for "yes"!

Long-Term Strategy

Oppose protracted campaigns and a strategy of quick decision, and uphold the strategy of protracted war and campaigns of quick decision.
—Chairman Mao

You may recall that in the 1970s and 1980s, much was made of the Japanese approach to business. The Japanese, it was said, focused on long-term goals and were willing to sacrifice profits in the short term in order to win market share. This was in stark contrast to typical Western, and especially American, thinking, which was geared to quarterly earnings reports and the wooing of fickle shareholders and the stock markets in general.

The Japanese economic miracle of the 1970s and 1980s, however, petered out. Economic crisis hit Japan, and for the first time since the end of World War II Japanese salarymen realized there was no guaranteed job for life at the major corporations. Japan is still an economic superpower, however, and to give the Japanese business strategy its due one has to admit that Japanese automakers dominate the American landscape (for instance). They have made their mark . . . and their market share.

The nice thing about SMEs in the United States and elsewhere is that they often are not listed on any stock exchange; they have no faceless shareholders to satisfy and no quarterly earnings reports to await with fear and trembling. Often, these smaller companies are wholly owned by a single family. That does not mean they don't have fiscal obligations outside the company—mortgages, small-business loans, and so forth—but that the decision-making powers rest in a single individual or small group of individuals. Such a company can afford to take a longer view, because their CEOs are not beholden to anyone outside their own companies. When share prices are not an issue, freedom ensues: freedom to make decisions, and to recover from them quickly if the decisions were poor ones. Further, not having a huge war chest to dig into means that short-term sales strategies and blitzkrieg-like marketing campaigns are alien to the way an SME does business. They simply don't have the cash flow. Instead, they will rely on longer-term strategies that use a smaller, but steadier, supply of funds to finance their overseas mission. In the end, this works better because the Chinese are naturally suspicious of flashy advertising campaigns by foreign companies and would prefer to see a representative of a foreign company on a regular basis, if not actually living in China then visiting frequently and regularly. The personal approach is valued over the impersonal sales and marketing campaign that puts products ahead of people.

Of course, advertising is still important and the Chinese are reassured by ubiquitous ads. Brand-name recognition is important in every market, of course; in China, it has another advantage.

Due to tight government controls over foreign currency reserves and suspicion of corrupt activity by companies eager to do business with the West, many Chinese are reluctant to deal with an unknown company. Should the business prove unsatisfactory for any reason, the person who supported the unknown company will be blamed. There will be hints of corruption, charges of incompetence, and worse. In some cases in the past where a business transaction has gone awry—products not delivered, or not delivered on time, or of substandard quality, etc.—the Chinese staffers who supported the unknown company have wound up in prison. However, if the foreign company is well known then officials will be reluctant to put all the blame on one person. It will be easier to blame the foreign company that placed all the advertising, proclaiming the high quality and excellent service of its firm, as being itself dishonest or deceptive. However, if the foreign company has other projects in China, successfully completed, then it will be that much easier for everyone to make the decision in its favor and no one will be blamed if it doesn't work out right. No one, that is, except you.

Thus, there is a tendency in Chinese companies to try to spread the responsibility for decision-making as much as possible. Partly, this is a legacy of Communism. I remember one particular case, in Baoding, after I had supervised the installation of some electrical equipment in a rayon plant. The equipment in question had been manufactured by a General Electric plant in Erie, Pennsylvania. The installation engineer was an Irishman who specialized in overseas engineering projects for GE. But the responsibility for the installation itself was, of course, that of the factory and its own engineers.

Once the installation had been completed, we wanted to test the equipment to make sure everything was hooked up correctly and there were no mistakes made in the wiring. It was to be a simple question of turning a switch. However, we were stopped at that point by the factory director.

A meeting took place on the factory floor. Everyone who had been involved in the project was now in a group huddle, making the decision to turn the switch or not, and whose responsibility it would be to actually turn the switch. Remember, this was not an official ribbon-cutting ceremony; we simply had to put some power into the equipment and check the gauges, but the decision had to be made by the group. Eventually, after more than twenty minutes of group discussion, the engineers stood up and told us we could proceed!

Since the group had made the decision, no single individual could be held accountable for any failure of the equipment once power was applied. It was a nervous moment for the Chinese side of the equation, and they wanted to ensure that everyone was on board with this final step in the installation process because it would be written up in a dozen small notebooks that they carried and they wanted to be sure that everyone was on the same page . . . literally.

What does this anecdote have to do with long-term strategy versus short-term marketing campaigns? The short-term approach is superficial, flashy, and aggressive. It requires a lot of cash, a lot of coordination, and in the end will not result in immediate sales but only in a general idea of the company and its products. It is an attempt to create confidence in the Chinese customer through artificial—i.e., impersonal—means. It does not satisfy a Chinese purchaser who has a dozen other considerations on his or her mind, not the least of which is prison time! A long-term approach, based on developing trust and confidence in your clients through personal "face time"—but supplemented with some advertising and marketing, especially in trade publications and at trade shows and exhibitions—goes a long way to getting those engineers on the factory floor to pull the switch that applies power to your sales mission.

What Box?

Some people hold a wrong view, which we refuted long ago. They say that it is enough merely to study the laws of war in general, or, to put it more concretely, that it is enough merely to follow the military manuals published by the reactionary Chinese government or the reactionary military academies in China. They do not see that these manuals give merely the laws of war

in general and moreover are wholly copied from abroad, and that if we copy and apply them exactly without the slightest change in form or content, we shall be "cutting the feet to fit the shoes" and be defeated.

—Chairman Mao

I cringe when I write the phrase "outside the box" because it has been overused and abused so often it has nearly lost its meaning. No one wants to be accused of thinking "inside the box" because that implies rigid thinking, uncreative approaches, and old-fashioned values. Yet, when it comes to business and spending money on foreign sales missions, that is exactly what comes to the fore. Fear of the unknown forces many companies into a defensive mode; they want to overcontrol a situation to the point where their sales executives can't think clearly, so worried are they that their actions will be scrutinized, criticized, and demonized.

That doesn't mean that the China trader should operate without constraint. He's not Colonel Kurtz in *Apocalypse Now!*, after all. There has to be a policy in place that protects the company from serious financial loss, from lawsuits, from illegality and charges of corrupt practices. However, as Mao rightly pointed out, the commander in the field has to be able to change standard operating procedure when the situation demands it, and do so quickly.

Mao rewrote the book on guerrilla warfare. He realized that guerrilla operations held many advantages over standard military units, but that they also had some built-in weaknesses. Mao re-imagined guerrilla warfare in the context of a people's revolution. It was not a matter of only relying on those civilian populations that were already on his side; he wanted to convert those who were neutral or even hostile to his campaign. He wanted to fire them up with dreams of a liberated China, a China governed not by foreign powers but by the Chinese themselves.

Furthermore, he demonstrated to them that such a dream was attainable in their lifetimes, and with that he earned their support. He was not only a military leader, he was also—in a sense—a kind of evangelist. In other words, a salesman.

Is There a "Box"?

In Chinese companies—whether in China itself or among the overseas Chinese communities of Singapore, Malaysia, Taiwan, San Francisco, and New York, to name but a few—the "box" is really only their shared cultural values. When it comes to doing business, business models are constantly being changed, amended, tested, discarded, redeveloped, re-created. Chinese businessmen realize that the goal is what is important, not the means of getting there. If a given corporate policy does not work, or a treasured sales strategy is failing, it is revisited and often either changed dramatically or discarded outright. Although a Chinese executive may be nominally in charge of the company he runs, information can come to him from every level of the corporate hierarchy and he will make changes in corporate direction due to new information he receives. And this can happen on a dime. Just as war gives us constantly shifting battle lines, so does business. Chinese companies are set up to be much more reactive than Western firms. Networking among Chinese companies—and between individuals in those companies—is a constant source of new information, new intelligence, and new opportunities. Chinese firms are not monolithic, but are rather much more horizontal in structure than vertical. The "box" as we know it does not exist in the average Chinese corporate culture. Instead, loyalty to family comes first, along with loyalty to the profit motive that benefits and enriches the family. Loyalty to a company is rare; a company, after all, is not a person. Chinese business executives see Westerners who are loyal to their company regardless of how the company treats them or the profitability of the company as people living inside the box.

Mao eschewed all forms of personal attachments to leaders or plans as decadent and individualistic. Mao was a pragmatist who felt that idealism was unreliable. He was results-driven; although his dream was a united and free China, he had no illusions about how he had to get there. He knew he was in for a long, protracted struggle. And while he felt that Communism held the key to his people's liberation and subsequent happiness, he did not romanticize the notion. He knew that the Russian Revolution held important lessons for his own struggle, but he also knew that the circumstances in Russia in 1917 were not identical to those in China in 1937. He knew when and how to make changes to the Party line when adhering to the Soviet model would be counterproductive.

This eminently realistic attitude to conflict is reflected in the ideas and attitudes of many of the Chinese decision-makers you will meet today. Idealism is a luxury they cannot afford; they smile at what they perceive to be the naiveté of Westerners who think they can be successful in China trade while at the same time keeping their hands scrupulously clean, free from any taint of sin or corruption. Just as for Chairman Mao there was no "box" during his revolutionary struggle for an independent China, there is no "box" for the Chinese company struggling for its own economic independence. If you want to succeed in China, you will have to emulate the local business practices that involve intense social engineering, social networking, and interpersonal relations. You will have to "build popular support," plan for the long term, "live off the land," and stay mobile and flexible. You do not have the luxury of becoming a legend in your own mind: today's success can just as easily be followed by tomorrow's failure. There is no time in China to rest on your laurels or to congratulate yourself on your accomplishments. You are a guerrilla fighter, always prone to betrayal, deception, and the influence of forces greater than those at your command. You have to stay lean and mean, otherwise what happened to Chairman Mao could just as easily happen to you, and then you go from being Good Mao to degenerating into Bad Mao.

Good Mao versus Bad Mao

Good Mao was in his element during his struggle against the forces of the Guomindang (Kuomintang, the Nationalist Chinese forces under Generalissimo Chiang Kai Shek). A brilliant tactician, Mao was able to run circles around the more formally organized Nationalist troops. And, when he was on the ropes and hurting from the continual pressure of Nationalist military might, he simply took a walk. The walk became known as the Long March, and it saved Mao's forces from being decimated, allowing him to regroup and go on the offensive again.

Bad Mao found himself unable to cope with the success of his revolution. Fearful of losing power, paranoid about the designs other countries (external forces) had on China, and worried that power struggles in his own Party and elsewhere within China (internal forces) would prove a threat to his leadership, he made impossible and quixotic demands on his own people. He had his farmers—the backbone of China's livelihood and survival—switch to smelting iron ore during the Great Leap Forward; the result was widespread famine. He purged his Party of suspiciously capitalist or democratic impulses and sent his intelligentsia—his brain capital—to the countryside to dig ditches and plant rice during the Cultural Revolution. He alienated his best and brightest, and called in the Army (and the fanatically devoted cadres) anytime he felt threatened. The goal became not to save the country, but to save Mao himself.

Bad Maoism in business means losing sight of the ultimate goal, which has to be profitability for your company. It also means sacrificing the enthusiasm and motivation of your personnel on the altar of egotism and vanity . . . or worse, on the killing field of corporate policy and the doctrine of "this is how we have always done things." Corporate policy is a tool, not a way of life or a substitute for religion or culture. If corporate policy does not further your business, it has to be amended. In China, "Marxism-Leninism and Mao Ze Dong Thought" was corporate policy; cadres quoted from Mao's speeches like the Devil quoting Scripture. And many perished because of it, like heretics at the stake. Those who survived lost their willingness to help promote China's growth and security. They lost their faith.

If that happens to your staff, you have lost the war. In a guerrilla environment like China during the Revolution, the enthusiasm and commitment of Mao's troops was sometimes the only resource they had. Starving, outnumbered, and outgunned, their idealism and faith in their principles and their leader made them stick it out until victory was assured. In business, the commitment and dedication of your staff—especially in China trade, the most volatile and potentially dangerous of the world's major markets—is essential. Further, that kind of commitment and dedication is contagious, not only among the rest of your company but among your clients, too. Your customers in China can smell a loser a kilometer away.

> **No military leader is endowed by heaven with an ability to seize the initiative. It is the intelligent leader who does so after a careful study and estimate of the situation and arrangement of the military and political factors involved.**
>
> **—Chairman Mao**

Good Mao is pragmatic and seeks alternate routes to victory. Good Mao never competes according to ideas and strategies handed down by others; he relies on good intelligence from the field, he surveys the landscape, he calculates his resources and estimates the cost of each victory in advance. If a time-worn approach will win, of course he will employ it. If it does not, it is rejected outright and another approach considered, designed, invented. If certain strategies ensured victory, after all, they would be used by everyone and there would be no losses.

Bad Mao forgets everything he learned in the field and tries to consolidate his power base using the same tired imperial concepts that he fought against his entire life. Bad Mao becomes his own enemy, fat with victory and oblivious to the changing forces around him. The CEO of an American or European company assumes that the business practices he or she employed in running the firm—including domestically oriented sales and marketing techniques—would work just as well overseas, from Turin to Tianjin. That's Bad Mao thinking: "I will keep the revolution going against my own people until all my enemies are dead and there is nothing left. If we need steel, why, everyone will make steel! If someone has an idea different from mine, they will be sent to the camps!" We all know there are CEOs like that; they may function domestically, but overseas they are a disaster. The problem is, like the Bad Mao, they will blame their failures on their personnel, or on the people overseas; on corruption, on disloyalty, on incompetence. They will never accept the blame, never re-evaluate their own policies or actions.

> **Dispersion, concentration, constant change of position—it is in these ways that guerrillas employ their strength.**
>
> **—Chairman Mao**

In the field, Good Mao had to constantly re-evaluate his position, constantly reform his strategy, constantly invent new tactics . . . all the while remaining true to his basic ideals and the ultimate goal of victory over the forces of the Nationalist Chinese. And he won.

In the pages that follow, we will look at some specific examples of his strategy and his thought and apply them to doing business in general but especially in China. We will also look at his mistakes, so that we can try to avoid them ourselves, of course, but also to understand modern China, the New China, and the personality and culture of the people we will meet: our New Customers.

Chapter 2
The Second Stratagem

Make what is old serve the new; make what is foreign serve China.

—Chairman Mao

Your first business trip to China will be crucial. The mistakes you make during this trip can haunt you for years to come, or, worse, you will never know what mistakes you made and will continue on, oblivious to the repercussions of your boorishness until it is too late.

We will talk about what to expect at this early stage in the book because you will have a chance to employ these techniques before you ever leave your home country. Should you form a partnership with a Chinese agent or sales representative, what you read in this chapter will help you negotiate your way through the tricky shoals of Chinese etiquette and raise the agent's comfort level even as you stabilize your *modus operandi.*

The crux of this approach lies in two, very important, concepts:

First, you are a foreigner. Even in your own country. Even in the United States. Or Canada. Or Germany. Or Australia, or anywhere else on the globe. To a Chinese businessperson, you will always be referred to as a "foreigner" (usually behind your back, or in your face if he or she is speaking a Chinese dialect). Get used to it.

The words for "foreigner" in Mandarin are *wai guo ren*, which mean, quite simply, "foreign country person." That's the polite form, even if its use is derogatory the way we use terms like "alien." Other ways of describing you and your parentage may include *gwei lo*, which is Cantonese for "white ghost." There is also "foreign devil" and all sorts of other terminology in a wide variety of Chinese languages, dialects, and inflections which denote your "other" status. To the Chinese of several hundred years ago, non-Chinese persons were simply not understood to be human: they were some form of supernatural life, the living dead perhaps, or the minions of some underworld country. The Chinese refer to their own country as the Middle Kingdom, which can be taken to mean either the center of the earth or the place between heaven and hell. However it is understood, be assured that you are a foreigner in it.

When I worked for Anthony Chang in downtown Manhattan, I was often referred to as *wai guo ren* even when I was in the room. This, from people who had been born in China while I was a native New Yorker, at home in my own city. The implication of this little fact of life is that, wherever you happen to be, if you are with Chinese people you are in China and are expected to behave as such.

Second, your ways—your values, your history, your experience, your culture—are never as important or interesting to your Chinese hosts or guests as their own. This is not snobbery or arrogance; it is simply a fact of life. The Chinese see themselves in terms of their own history, which is lengthy and spans millennia. In a Chinese timeline, one normally begins with the reign of the Three Sovereigns, which took place in the twenty-seventh century BCE. That's the year 2,700 BC. In other words, the Chinese have been doing business at least that long. Maybe longer. They know what they're doing. You are not going to teach them anything. So, the best thing you can do under the circumstances is shut up and smile.

Once these two concepts are understood—not enjoyed or embraced, perhaps, but understood—then one can proceed to the next phase of our re-education campaign: the business meeting.

The Business Meeting

I am going to explain this on the assumption that my reader is a typical Western businessperson, an American perhaps from the Midwest: someone who has been doing business for years, comfortable with the usual strategies and tactics of modern American business relationships. Small amendments may be necessary if you are from a different country and culture, but the overall approach will be quite familiar in any case. As someone who has brought many European as well as American companies to China, I can state that Europeans are somewhat easier to introduce to Chinese business etiquette than Americans for the simple reason that Europeans—living on a continent that enables them to go from a French-speaking country to an Italian- or Spanish- or German- or Swedish- or Hungarian-speaking country (among many others) in a matter of hours *by car*—generally understand that there is a vast and complicated world outside their borders. Americans, sadly, are not usually aware of the differences that exist outside their borders, and if their first overseas assignment is China they are in for a very rude awakening.

An American businessperson will greet a guest with a hearty handshake, a big smile, a booming voice, and an expansive gesture. He (typically a "he") will pat the guest on the back, perhaps, and direct the guest to a chair that is set at a conference table. Business cards will be exchanged. Brochures passed around. Business discussed almost at once. Once the business discussion has been concluded, the guest may be invited to lunch and preparations made to transport everyone to the nearest reasonably priced restaurant for some burgers and beer . . . or in this case, and if the host is particularly sensitive cultur-ally, to the nearest American Chinese restaurant for a meal of fried rice, chow mein and egg rolls, followed by a fortune cookie.

However, there are a number of problems with this approach and we have to dissect them carefully.

The Chinese are not ones for expansive gestures, loud voices, and glad-handing, particularly among strangers. All of that is considered vulgar. The Chinese are under-stated in their dealings with foreigners (and with each other). They smile, bow, and shake hands. Before anything else takes place, they will want to exchange business cards or "name cards": *ming pian* as they are called in Mandarin. This is a ritual, the first of many, and it is extremely impor-tant that it be executed correctly.

The Name Card Ritual

You must accept the guest's name card with *both* hands. This is a significant Chinese gesture and indicates that one needs both hands to accept such a weighty offering. It is how the Chinese accept gifts of any kind, with both hands and a slight bow. It shows respect for the person, and for the title and other information on the card. In a culture where *guanxi*—connections—are vitally important, a name card is like a key to a node in the social network.

When you accept the card, look at it. Actually *read* it. Note the person's name, title, company name, address, everything. Show respect for the person by paying close attention to the card.

When you proffer your own card, you must follow this procedure:

Hold the card with both hands, the same way as described above. Make sure that the card faces the person you are giving it to, so that they don't have to turn it around to read it. They will accept it with both hands and a slight bow, and they will read it.

Do not—I repeat, do *not*—put the card you have just received into your pocket and forget about it! The card should remain on the desk or conference table in front of you at all times during the meeting. If there are several Chinese guests at this meeting you will thank me for this advice. I have a practice which has served me well over the years, and it consists of placing the business cards in front of me matching how the Chinese are seated on the other side of the desk or table. Thus, if Mr. Wong is seated on my far right, his business card is the first one on the right in front of me, followed by those of Mr. Li, Ms. Zhao, and Mr. Hu, in the order they are seated, with Mr. Hu seated at the far left and his card on the far left. This way I can associate the unfamiliar names with their faces and their titles, and know who is saying what and what title they have.

You must not collect these cards from the table until the meeting is over, at which point you collect them carefully and respectfully.

If you and your associates are already in the conference room when the Chinese guests arrive, do not do something I have seen done so many times that it's simply no longer funny: do not, under any circumstances, deal your business cards around like you are dealing from a deck of playing cards! Follow the above instructions and hand each Chinese person your business card with both hands, one by one, and receive them the same way. It takes longer this way, but it's the only way to do this without offending anyone and, anyway, the Chinese are not ones to rush through a business meeting. After more than four thousand years of doing business, they can afford to take a little longer to get to know you and size you up, which is what they are doing when they are performing the name card ritual and what you should be doing as well.

Sitting Down

Once the ritual has been performed, you direct the Chinese to their seats at the table. They will not sit until you sit, so when everyone is at their assigned place you can ask them to be seated and then you sit down. The same will happen in reverse: if you are the guest of a

Chinese host—in China or anywhere else—they will wait until you are at your seat and everyone is standing around the table and then they will beg you to sit, at which point you can.

However . . . they may ask you to sit down before everyone else has positioned themselves. In that case, smile but remain standing until everyone else is ready. That shows breeding. Often, the Chinese will direct you to a specific seat; there is usually a reason for this, and I recommend you follow their seating recommendations. One reason may be that they wish to seat you directly across from the person who most closely duplicates your own corporate position. Thus, if you are the CEO of your company, they will seat you directly across from their own CEO or factory director or general manager. They will not fuss so much about everyone on your side, but they will identify the major players and structure the seating accordingly.

Often, there will be quite a few Chinese persons at any meeting, especially those taking place in China. Rarely will you be meeting a Chinese businessperson alone. Across from you will be people with various responsibilities in the company you are visiting, from the factory director to several engineers, business managers, and even the local Communist Party official just to make sure the proceedings are in accordance with doctrine. If the Chinese are visiting you in your own country—on a factory inspection, perhaps—there will be a number of them, usually one person who can make decisions, an engineer or two, and perhaps one or two persons whose function is not so easily defined: in the old days, this latter would include at least one Communist Party member to keep an eye on the others and ensure they did not defect. That person was usually in charge of everyone's passports. Today, it might mean someone from the company who is just along for the ride because it is her or his turn to travel abroad. They will have name cards, however, so there will be some indication as to their status and area of responsibility.

A Matter of Interpretation

Many Chinese speak some English, and some speak other languages as well. However, an interpreter is not only desirable in every business meeting but should be considered an absolute requirement. The way of handling the interpretation is also a matter of etiquette, mixed with common sense.

If the only interpreter at the meeting is the one working for the Chinese, then you can expect several things to happen. In the first place, the quality of the interpretation may not be first-rate: many interpreters in China are recent college graduates who majored in English and who therefore cannot manage much more than "Hello" and "Goodbye" in polite conversation. I'm not casting aspersions here; how many American graduates who studied Spanish or French can actually handle themselves in Spain or France? Often, these younger Chinese interpreters are pretty good when it comes to written English—well, okay, some of them anyway—but not when it comes to actually speaking it or understanding your own particular regional accent. Even if they are relatively fluent in conversational English, they may not understand complicated technical jargon and mistranslate those terms with reckless abandon. They may also get numbers wrong: the Chinese system of counting is different from that used in the States, and it is easy to misplace a decimal position or two during translation, which can have horrendous consequences, as I am sure you can imagine!

In the second place, a Chinese interpreter may not translate everything you say or everything the other side says. This may be due to reluctance to translate something they feel may be rude or impolite; or it may be due to instructions from their employers not to translate some critical piece of information or a particularly telling observation they have just made. A Chinese interpreter may not be able to translate the nuance of a conversation, and this is usually where the action is.

Therefore, I make the following recommendations:

Have your own translator—one you have hired who is working only for you—with you at every business meeting with the Chinese. (Some astute readers will ask, "How can you be sure the translator is working only for you?" The answer to that, of course, is: you can't, especially if you hired the translator locally, in China. The best solution is to bring one with you from your own country, but that can be prohibitively expensive.)

Provide the translator—either your own, or the translator for the other side, or both—a list of key technical terms and jargon at least a day in advance. This will enable them to look up the meanings in a Chinese technical dictionary so they will not be blindsided during the meeting.

Pay close attention to what is being translated. Often, you can tell that a long sentence of yours has been reduced to a few syllables. This means that the translator has, for some reason, not translated your exact words. This is either due to a lack of understanding or to some other reason having to do with the lack of interest of your opposite numbers. Repeat the sentence, perhaps using a slightly different way to say the same thing, but without getting impatient or angry with the translator or letting on that you know there is a problem. You will see a light go on in the translator's eyes, and your words will find a home.

When it comes to numbers, don't hesitate to write them down for the translator as you are speaking. This makes it easy to avoid a mistranslation. For instance, the Chinese normally do not translate the number 100,000 as "one hundred thousand" but as "ten ten thousands." Thus, when you say "one hundred thousand" it may get mistranslated as 10,000 or something else. If you write the number down, however, and show it to your translator as you speak, this problem is avoided.

When speaking through a translator, do not look at him or her. You are not speaking *to* the translator, but *through* the translator. It is a very common error to speak during a business meeting as if the translator is the factory director or the CEO; I've seen seasoned professionals make that mistake. It is, however, quite rude and also tactically poor. You want to engage your opposite number, and you can only do that with body language and eye contact. Look directly at the person you are addressing, even if you know they don't understand a word you're saying. And when they are speaking to you in their own language look straight at *them* and not at the translator. If you have seen still or film footage of meetings between heads of state— for instance, in the White House—you will note that the translators sit *behind* the chairs of the President and the Prime Minister. They are heard, but not seen. That is the optimal way to use an interpreter.

The Negotiation

Typically, every business negotiation consists of two parts: the technical aspect of the products or services being sold, and the commercial details: pricing, delivery, etc. The Chinese business negotiation is no different, and in fact is even more strenuous and complex than a similar negotiation taking place in a Western country. That is because the Chinese do not completely trust *wai guo ren* to live up to their word. Mao has told them that they are surrounded by enemies: the capitalists without, and the capitalist-roaders within. While capitalism is no longer the dirty word in China that it used to be, foreigners are still suspect. Again, this is partly due to Chinese history—the Opium Wars come to mind—and partly due to Chinese xenophobia. Remember that Chinese often refer to non-Chinese as "foreign devils" or "white ghosts"; while few Chinese today actually believe these designations, the ideas they represent nonetheless function as a kind of built-in warning system when it comes to dealing with people with whom they do not share a common heritage, language, or set of customs.

What this means in practice is simple: you have to prove yourself and your company and its products or services to the Chinese to an extent you would not be expected to do back home. Before the Chinese will entrust you with a single *yuan*, they will want to be assured that they will get value for money. Gone are the days when a smiling foreign face from America or Europe was easy entrée into the world of Chinese business. What the Chinese want now is be absolutely certain that you and your company can be relied upon to deliver and to follow up . . . and to be there a year from now, five years from now, to answer for any defaults or defects and to resupply with spare parts, training, and other aftermarket requirements as they come up.

Since they can't see into the future any more than you can, they have come up with methods to enlarge their comfort zone when it comes to dealing with foreign firms. The first method takes place during the technical discussion.

If you are selling to the Chinese, be prepared—be very prepared—for this aspect of the negotiation. There is literally nothing the Chinese will not ask you about your product and you will be amazed at how much you don't know about your own merchandise. Many Chinese youth wound up going to engineering school because it was the least politically suspect of any college subject. Foreign languages were out, because of the assumption that one who could read English or French or Spanish—for instance— would become contaminated by Western ideas and Western decadence or, even worse, could lead to allegations that one was spying for the West. Subjects such as political science, history, philosophy, etc. were equally dangerous. In science and engineering, however, there is no room for Western spiritual pollution. Hard sciences are just that: hard. They require attention to detail, computing capability, and knowledge of facts and data that cannot be refuted or "interpreted." Engineering was, and remains, the safest subject to study in China.

This has lead to many companies being top-heavy and bottom-heavy with engineers. Some of these engineers specialize in antique technology, such as the internal combustion engine. Others spent have their lives studying the metric system, torque, or the composition of paint. Thus, when they show up at your factory—or you at theirs—you will be expected to know absolutely everything there is to know about your product or process. And you won't. It just is not possible.

Let's say, for instance, that you are selling a computer system. You feel reasonably certain you can discuss bits and bytes with the best of them. You know where your chips came from, and how the motherboard was constructed. You even designed part of the system yourself. What could go wrong?

One of the engineers will ask you about the metal frame of the computer. How thick is it in millimeters? What type of aluminum? How was it painted? With what chemical composition of paint? How much heat is generated by the computer and how does that affect the paint in terms of fumes measured in parts per million? What is the decibel level of the noise generated by the fan inside the computer? Can this level be lowered? By how much? What is the life expectancy of the fan? What screws are used in attaching the fan to the frame? How many screws? How many threads per inch does each screw have? Of what material is the screw?

And you haven't even discussed the actual processing power of the computer yet.

This is a typical Chinese technical discussion, unfortunately. You have to be prepared for it. Because you cannot be expected to answer all of these questions with any degree of competence you better have some people on your staff who can. Before any such meeting, spend at least a week or more preparing all the necessary background information on every aspect of your product or process. In the case of complicated systems such as plastic or rubber extrusion lines, sheet metal lines, wire or cable lines, etc. the amount of information you need to have at your fingertips will be enormous, in which case a week will not be enough. You will have to have specifications for each machine in the production line (and remember that this includes such details as the type of paint, the composition of the steel used to make the machine, the decibel levels emitted by the machine, the amount of water, oil, electricity, and other consumables required for its operation, and so on, and so on . . . ad infinitum, ad nauseam). You will need to have operating manuals for each machine, as well as for the complete production line. If the production line uses computer software (for process controls, etc.) you will need to have this software available for demonstration and someone competent to discuss the software itself: what type of operating system, what type of machines will it run on, who wrote it, what version or revision it represents, how it may be modified by the Chinese (Will they be able to use Chinese language monitors and screens, for instance, or Chinese language keyboards?).

At the same time, you must be aware of the environmental issues at the locality where your equipment will be installed. Many places in China—particularly in rural areas where many factories are located—do not have adequate or reliable electrical power or water or heat or air-conditioning, etc. That is why some of their questions may sound absurd to you, but they may mask other concerns of which you could not possibly be aware. During the technical presentation, you can try to gain some information from the customer about the conditions of the site where your product will be installed, but it will be difficult to get a firm, unambiguous answer to your questions. They will insist that you simply present all the technical specifications of your product first. They may, if time allows—and it often will not—give you some information about the installation site, but that is rare at this stage. Instead, you will have to make the trip to the site yourself and spend a few days in the town to observe the plant's operation. You will be able to glean some important data on electrical power—brownouts, blackouts, and power-rationing are common in many parts of China, which can wreak havoc with delicate electronic equipment—and raw material supply.

We will go into this aspect of doing business in China in more detail in Chapter Seven, but for now let me refer to one case I was involved with in the mid-1980s. We had sold a complete production line for the manufacture of rubber hose. It was a state-of-the-art system, with advanced process controls, a molten salt curing bath that ran forty feet in length, and high-speed extruders. We were not aware, however, that the plant had no electrical power for a day or so each week. What that meant was they turned the power off on the molten salt bath, which solidified the salt (especially in the cold, north China winters) and when they turned the salt bath back on it distorted the curing tanks so badly they reared up like a python attacking a water buffalo, ripping them off the floor with the middle part of the production line suspended in mid-air!

Once the technical aspects of your product have been exhausted to the customer's satisfaction, you will be expected to sign off on them. Basically, that means that a complete set of specifications will be agreed upon by everyone there. It will be typed up, copies made for everyone, and the principals on both sides will sign the document. That does not mean you have the sale, of course, just that the specs have been determined and you have agreed to provide equipment that will meet every single item on the document you have just signed. The Chinese *will* go over that document thoroughly, especially every time they believe you have not lived up to your part of the agreement.

In addition, you have probably already noticed that the Chinese are taking copious notes all during your technical presentation. In many cases, they are actually writing down everything you say so that they can hang you with your own words later, if need be. The fact that more than one person is writing all this down means that they have backup: if two or more Chinese have written the same thing, then it can be assumed to be true and not the result of a misunderstanding or typographical error, etc. Thus, be careful of what you say during the technical presentation. Whatever you do say "can and will be used against you" by the customer, especially if they are not happy with the way things go later.

Once everyone has agreed to the technical specs, you will proceed to the commercial part of the negotiation.

This is also not as easy as it sounds, and the negotiation contains several pitfalls. I have worked out a strategy to deal with these, so please take the following suggestions very seriously.

In the West, a contract is a contract. Quite often, we sign a sales contract and then never look at it again. We deal in good faith with our customers, and they deal in good faith with us. However, in China, there is no good faith where foreign firms are concerned. The assumption is that you are either incompetent, or stupid, or dishonest. At best, you are too clever by half. The Chinese will build some protection into the contract, and you have to know how this works.

In the old days (the 1980s and 1990s) and to some extent today, the Chinese see the contract as an opportunity. *You are never finished negotiating the contract*, no matter that you have already shipped and installed the merchandise as agreed upon according to the terms and conditions in every scrap of paper you have signed. Be aware. Beware.

First, you must quote an initial figure that is quite high because the Chinese will *never* take your first price. You may not bargain much in the States or in Europe for your products or services, but in Asia you will and most especially in China. Therefore, your asking price must be close to double what you are comfortable with. Don't worry, it will come down to a level you are most definitely *not* comfortable with!

As part of the contract price you will note that often you will be asked to host a Chinese delegation for a week or so, for "training" or for "factory inspection" or some such excuse. You will be expected to pick up the tab for this, especially if your contract price is somewhere in the millions but this codicil can appear even if your total contract price is in the mid-$100,000s. You will bargain over the number of people you will host, and for how long. In some cases, you will even be providing the delegation with some "pocket money" that they will use to buy souvenirs . . . or appliances. This is not bribery or corruption (We will discuss that later!), but is part of the purchase price; i.e., the customer is actually paying for this because it is included in the contract price. You just were not expecting it, and now your profit margin has shrunk a little.

Another hidden cost is the holdback.

Often, especially when dealing in letters of credit, your payment schedule will be broken down into stages. You will get a down payment of perhaps twenty or thirty percent of the total contract value. You will get another amount—perhaps another thirty percent—when you ship the goods and provide the necessary shipping documentation to the bank that is holding the letter of credit. You will get another percentage after the equipment arrives in China and is inspected. And then there will be ten percent left over.

This holdback is a bargaining ploy. After the equipment has arrived, and been installed, and the operators trained in the equipment, and there is nothing left to do, you will be expecting this ten percent to arrive like clockwork in your account. It won't. In order to retrieve any part of that ten percent you will have to go to China and renegotiate.

Your customer will have photographs. You will see a damaged container. Some rust on a machine. A loose screw, and I don't mean in his head. You will have a report that someone was not trained quite so thoroughly, or that some promised spare parts did not arrive, or arrived short, or arrived in the wrong color. You will have little or no way to prove the truth or falseness of these claims, but that is not why you're there.

If you were smart, you built that ten percent into your costings during the commercial negotiations and can live without ever seeing it. If the contract price is high enough, though, it would behoove you to try to recoup as much of it as possible, particularly as not to do so will look suspicious to the Chinese, who will believe they have been snookered. So, you will fly to China and spend another three or four days on-site, listening to the pro forma Chinese complaints, smiling, nodding politely, clucking your way through the photographs, and finally agreeing upon a price. They will try to keep the entire ten percent, of course, but they don't really expect they will. You will present some counterarguments and, in the spirit of doing business together again some day, will agree to recouping maybe five percent of the original ten. Maybe even seven percent. If you do, of course, you will have shown your company that you have what it takes to do China trade because that last percentage is the most difficult part of the contract negotiation to win.

Often, the holdback will not be based on an event—such as a successful installation or operation of the equipment—but on a time factor: such as one year after the installation in order to be certain that everything works as promised. The above still applies, however: you will have to return to China to fight for every decimal place of that ten percent. And good luck to you!

Leaving the Room

This is going to sound awfully silly, but there is also some basic etiquette to be observed when the meeting is over and you are getting ready to leave the conference room. Everyone stands, and then your hosts will guide you to the door. This is where many foreigners make a mistake, one that is considered rather rude. They simply leave.

If you want to impress your Chinese counterparts with your good breeding and fine manners, you will insist that they leave the room before you. You have just scored one point. They will be suitably impressed, and then they will show you the door once more. You will refuse and insist they go first. They will refuse and insist you go first.

What I do—and I can get away with this because I am a naturally self-effacing kind of guy—is refuse to go first under any circumstances. That means that my opposite number will then take me by the arm, physically, and attempt to propel me through the door. I am not making this up. At that time, I then grab his arm and try to do the same. This results in much general mirth. Eventually, one of us goes first through the door but only after a few moments of this physical comedy. What that does, though, is make everyone feel a lot better about having hosted that foreign devil because he obviously had a Chinese nanny in there somewhere who taught him how to go through a door the right way.

You don't have to be so dramatic, but you do have to insist—at least for awhile—that your host (or guest) goes through the door first. If possible, you can go through together. But at least try. You get points for that, and the goodwill you will create by this very respectful gesture will go a long way toward improving your profile with your customers.

The Banquet

Eating is an important social event for the Chinese. A lot of business is done at the dinner table, even though business is not actually discussed. The Chinese want to see you as a person. After all, they do not buy from companies but from people. If they don't trust you as a person you are not likely to win any contracts. They want to know that you are a decent human being, and one way to learn that is to eat with you and see how you behave.

Much of what can be said about Chinese banquet etiquette is basic to any well-mannered person anywhere in polite society. However, I have watched as new generations of Americans have grown up with few or no social graces, as even the older generation has forgotten how to navigate a formal occasion. Therefore, the following remarks.

You will not avoid being asked to a formal Chinese banquet, even if "formal" means the factory's own cafeteria or a local restaurant that looks as if it was the last holdout in a condemned building. Remember that China is a country that is still largely rural and agrarian: a necessity when you have to feed more than one billion people. Unless you are luxuriating in Beijing or Shanghai, then, you will be dining at an establishment chosen by your hosts that may not appear to be particularly elegant but the food will most likely be succulent . . . if somewhat unfamiliar.

Your hosts will probably organize the banquet on the first evening; you will be expected to reciprocate the following evening. Never fear, your hosts can arrange that for you, too. You simply tell them how many people you would like to invite, and they will take it from there. All you will have to do is pay for everything, which is not as bad as it sounds.

When you enter the banquet room, you will see at least one round table and possibly more. Usually, this type of affair calls for two round tables: one for the honored guests and one for other staff whose turn it was to eat out that night.

If you are the guest, you must not—under any circumstances—sit down at the table until your host is there at his seat insisting you sit. Your host will occupy the seat at the head of the table. How do you know what seat is at the head of a round table? Quite simply, it's the seat facing the door. You will probably sit at either the host's right or left, with other members of your foreign delegation sitting on the other side, with more important Chinese guests interspersed among you. If you have some lower-echelon people with you, there is a good chance that at least one of them will be sitting at the other round table. Not to worry. If they have read this book and learned what is in it, they will comport themselves in a way guaranteed to bring honor and glory upon your head.

Second rule: you do not eat a single morsel of food, nor drink a single sip of any liquid, until your host begins. In fact, you must not lift your glass unless you are prepared to give a toast or partake in a toast. Drinking is as serious as eating at a Chinese banquet, and you must observe the formalities.

At a formal Chinese banquet you will see three glasses before you. The first, quite small, is for *mao tai*: the overproof firewater that smells like formaldehyde and has quite a kick. The second is a wine glass and is usually used for a very sweet red wine, more like a sherry or a port than a cabernet. The third is a large water glass but, alas, it is not used for water but for beer. Often, all three will be filled and the people making the toasts will lift one and you will be expected to drink from the same size glass.

That means, in effect, that you will be mixing beer, wine, and *mao tai* throughout the evening. Lucky for you, you will also be eating, which will ameliorate the effects of all that alcohol somewhat.

Your host will probably make the first toast. At a Chinese toast, everyone stands and lifts their glass. The appropriate response is usually *Gan bei!*, which is Mandarin for "empty glass" and which means just that: you have to empty your glass. You prove that your glass is empty by holding it upside down after you've drunk the toast. You then put the glass back on the table and someone comes from somewhere and immediately refills it.

The night has just begun.

Everyone at your table will make a toast. If there are ten people sitting at your table, there will be ten toasts, ten *gan bei*'s. Of course, you are expected to make toasts as well and you will start with toasting your host. After an appropriate interval of munching sea cucumber in oyster sauce or shredded pork or pickled vegetables, you will then toast someone else at the table (not, of course, your own people). If the party is particularly jovial, you will wind up leaving your table after you have toasted everyone there and moving over to the other table and toasting the table in general. (You normally do not have to toast everyone individually at the second table.)

Make sure to keep eating, or the alcohol will take over. However, regardless of your best intentions, you will start to feel the effects of all that drinking eventually. No matter, so will your hosts. There will be joking, questions about life in your home country, and some very personal questions perhaps that under ordinary circumstances you would find rude: your age, your income, how many cars you own, things like that.

The first banquet with your Chinese customers will usually not end in a drunken revel. They don't know you well enough for that, yet. It will end appropriately early, and you will be escorted to your hotel. The Chinese will not simply drive you to your hotel and dump you on the sidewalk in front of it, though. They will get out of their cars and see you to the hotel entrance, shaking your hand and waving at you until you disappear into the building. Make a note of this, for you will be doing a lot of that yourself.

The second banquet is on you. You can have your customers arrange that for you, of course, and the only thing you have to worry about is paying for it at the end of the evening. The first night, your hosts paid and they usually did so out of your sight and hearing. The host himself would have stayed behind until you left in the company of your driver and whatever other of the Chinese group has been designated to see you get to your hotel safely. When it is your turn to pay, you will do the same: wait until your customers leave and then handle the transaction quietly.

At your banquet, you will be sitting at the round table facing the door, just like your counterpart did the previous evening. No one will lift a chopstick until you do, and no one will drink until you raise the first glass and make the first toast. Everything else will be the same and follow the same format. And when your guests get up to leave, you will stand and remain standing until they have left the room. In fact, you will accompany them to the door of your private dining room and stand in the doorway waving at them until they are completely out of sight, every last man and woman of them.

During every banquet, you will notice something which may seem a little peculiar. The gentleman or lady on your left or right will pick up something from one of the dishes in the center of the table and put it on your plate. This is an expression of kindness and graciousness, and it does not have to be reciprocated until you feel comfortable enough to do so. They will not use the chopsticks they eat with, however. They will use a "serving set" of chopsticks or perhaps one of the serving spoons that accompany the dishes. You probably already know that the Chinese eat "family style," which means all the dishes are set in the middle of the table—usually on a revolving "lazy Susan"—and everyone picks up a morsel and puts it on their plate and rotates the lazy Susan around to the next plate, etc. Usually, the banquet begins with cold appetizers such as pickled cucumber slices, duck claws, sliced meat of uncertain provenance, etc. It then proceeds to warmer dishes, usually seafood (such as giant prawns, sea cucumber if you rate it, tiny clams, etc.), and sometimes chicken or duck. You will rarely see beef or pork.

One appetizer that was very fashionable in China in the past few years is lobster sashimi. For this rather exquisite if initially unsettling dish, a live lobster has its tail "sashimied" Japanese style, with small saucers of soy sauce and wasabe mustard arrayed around it. The lobster arrives on a carved wooden "boat," and one uses one's chopsticks to pick up pieces of the tail and dip it in the appropriate sauce. Eventually, while enjoying this delicacy, you will notice with something akin to horror that the lobster is still alive. You will see its tentacles move, its claw raise languidly into the air before falling, and the lobster actually try to walk off the boat.

Another delicacy consists of small pigeons that have been deep-fried entire. They are served on a large platter intact, beaks and all. Still another is one of my favorites: drunken shrimp. The orthodox way of preparing this dish is to take a good handful of live shrimp and dump them into a bowl of cognac. The bowl is then covered, and the shrimp jump around in the cognac until they eventually stop moving. The cover is removed and . . . *bon appetit!* The taste is something between brine and brandy. In Southeast Asia, they prepare drunken shrimp the same way but once the shrimp have stopped moving they are taken away and steamed before being returned to the table, much to the relief of some who know how the dish was originally created, although after steaming it lacks a certain . . . *je ne sais quoi.*

You have all heard of the stories about monkey brains. I can honestly say I have never eaten monkey brains (not consciously, anyway), but there are a few dishes that do it one better. This is one that I learned about from my dear friend Peter Wong.

In South China—Guangdong Province, to be exact—there is a special, very expensive and very rare dish which is enjoyed only by those who have the wallet (and the stomach) for it. The method of preparation is simplicity itself.

One takes a pregnant rat.

The rat is brought to the table in a somewhat comatose state. The chef—Doctor Mengele, I presume—then injects the rat with a chemical that induces labor. The rat gives birth at the table to dozens of tiny baby rats. One picks up a baby rat, dips it into the array of sauces that are available, and . . . eats it. The going rate for this demonic delicacy was about three hundred US dollars the last time I checked.

The Chinese know that foreigners have no stomach for this stuff, and anyway it's too expensive a dish to waste on *you*, so you need have no worries that something that strange will appear at your table. Drunken shrimp, however, is a possibility. As is turtle, frog, and snake. The Chinese have a saying that they will eat anything that walks, crawls, swims, or flies. Or tries to get away. Some dishes even look like they have been shot while trying to escape.

Before you dismiss this attitude as barbaric, remember that we are dealing with a country that has known serious famine. During the reign of Mao Ze Dong, it is estimated that some twenty million Chinese died of starvation. In addition, most of China is not arable land. They cannot raise cows because there is not enough grazing land; the land has to be used for growing vegetables and rice. This means that one has to struggle to find sources of protein. There is pork, but not enough for all 1.2 billion people, of which a few million are Muslims who prefer mutton and cannot eat pork anyway. So, the people are reduced to finding their protein where they can: as frogs, turtles, snakes, various forms of seafood that we would not recognize such as the inimitable sea cucumber (really just a giant worm), squid, octopus, eel, etc. Also, let us not forget the insects.

One of my most memorable meals in China took place in 1986. My boss—Anthony Chang—and I were the guests of the governor of Shandong Province at a quiet, intimate dinner in a hotel in Tianjin. There was just the governor, his wife, the governor's aide, and the two of us.

The first, appetizer, course contained a local delicacy that I had never seen before. There, on a serving dish, was a mountain of tiny . . . scorpions. These were called "mountain scorpions" and I was assured that they were (no longer) poisonous. They had been deep-fried and had a crunchy, almost potato-chip-like, texture. They were complete, entire scorpions, however, with that unmistakable profile and the prominent stinger.

Many years later, when I was having a hard time with an engineer from the States who, was causing all sorts of havoc with my Beijing-based staff I had a little fun. Said engineer was averse to eating most of the food for which China is justly famous. He also did not drink, which in China is a kind of liability. Frustrated that he would not adapt to the social requirements expected of him and was, in the bargain, making life difficult for me and my staff, I decided to take my revenge in a rather understated way. I invited him to a restaurant that had just opened not far from his hotel.

Peter Wong had ordered in Mandarin while the engineer was busy reminding us that he did not eat this and that and the other thing. No problem. When the appetizer course arrived, it almost took my breath away.

Insects. Lots of them. Grasshoppers. Caterpillars. Ants. Scorpions. And the *piece de resistance*: silkworms! Each and every one of these insects was whole and intact. They had been sautéed, deep-fried, boiled . . . all manner of culinary skill had been expended in the execution of this memorable feast. The engineer turned several different shades of green, and then capitulated. As long as we did not make him eat the insects, he would eat whatever else it was we put in front of him. Thankfully for him he was on his way back home the following day.

Karaoke

When discussing the entertainment of customers in China, the question of karaoke inevitably comes up. It's a phenomenon with many different variations, and one should be aware of all of them, for the Chinese love their karaoke and no evening's entertainment is complete without a video monitor, a microphone, a song catalog, free-flowing alcohol . . . and, well, other things.

Karaoke was originally a Japanese invention. A melody is played over an audio-visual system with the lyrics of the song on the screen so you can sing along into a microphone. Amateur night.

In many clubs, you stand in front of a room full of total strangers and make a fool of yourself, belting out your tin-ear version of "Tie a Yellow Ribbon" or "Heartbreak Hotel." In China and many other parts of Asia, however, you have options.

When you are taking your customers out for karaoke, you normally go to a club that has private rooms. Each of these rooms is equipped with comfortable couches, your own private A-V system with large speakers, a huge catalog of available songs in Mandarin, Cantonese, English, and other languages, at least two or more microphones, and a menu of available beverages.

One can order a round of beers, of course, and often I have done just that. Usually, though, one orders a bottle or two of some overpriced alcohol, such as Hennessey or Martel XO or VSOP, Courvoisier, or maybe a bottle of Absolut. The Chinese seem to prefer cognac to most other alcoholic beverages and even drink it during dinner, something that takes us Westerners a little getting used to. Their tastes are changing, however, and the more adventurous among them have started drinking French wine and Scottish whiskey.

The attraction of karaoke, however, is not limited to singing and drinking. If you are out with an all-male group of Chinese customers, you are most likely going to wind up at any one of literally thousands of karaoke bars in China that double as prostitution centers.

Normally, there is no sexual activity taking place on the premises of these clubs. Instead, there is a manager (male or female, but most often female and sometimes referred to as a "mama san" in unselfconscious homage to old American films about post-War Japan) who assigns a hostess to your group. The hostess is just that: she takes the drink orders and makes sure everything is running smoothly in your private room.

In addition, there will be a number of ladies who will attend your group. Their job is to make sure that the alcohol flows and that the karaoke system is humming along nicely. They will play drinking games, talk to you (if they speak any English; at this point it is useful to know some Mandarin so you can at least pretend to have a conversation), and smile at you as if you were the most fascinating thing they have ever seen. Well, that night, anyway.

They are also often available as sexual partners, but this must take place off-site. You can make an arrangement for later that evening or even the next day or next evening, usually at your hotel. As a rule, there is no sexual activity allowed on the premises of the karaoke club for the simple reason that they get raided with regularity (particularly if they have not been dutiful in paying off the local constabulary or if their *guanxi*—their connections—are insufficient to protect them). Further, as you probably realize, prostitution is illegal in China and no karaoke owner wants to get hauled in front of a Chinese court where you are presumed guilty and must throw yourself on the mercy of the judges. Thus, you may make arrangements privately with the lady of your choice—which usually is nothing more than getting her phone or pager number—but you will not sleep with her that night.

There are exceptions, of course. There are a few—very few—clubs in Beijing and Shanghai where it is possible to enjoy the sexual favors of your lady of the evening *that* evening, but the cost is usually quite high. These clubs are generally either owned or under the protection of the Peoples Liberation Army or the Public Security Bureau. They will never be raided. However, it is extremely difficult to know which club is so protected from the outside; you need someone local you can rely upon who knows the lay of the land, so to speak.

I will not presume to moralize about this state of affairs. Morality is between you and your conscience . . . and your doctor. (The ladies are usually clean and free of STDs, especially in the more expensive clubs, but it would be suicidal to take a chance that they are; instead, the use of prophylactics is highly and most strenuously recommended!) You need not feel pressured to make an assignation with any of these ladies at any time. The fact that you are in the karaoke club with your Chinese customers and everyone is having a great time is good enough. You will not "lose face" if you refuse the company of one of these women later on; in fact, you can always take her phone number and simply not call her. She won't be disappointed: there are a lot of names in her little black book. The importance of the karaoke experience is, quite simply, male-bonding. If you, as a foreigner, can fit in with this most Asian of male-oriented experiences then you will have crossed another hurdle in gaining acceptance by your customers. A stiff attitude, however, will not win you any friends or influence any customers; whether or not you intend to engage the services of a lady of the evening, it is important that you show that you are not bothered at all about this and that it is all in good fun.

I have found that my European colleagues are much more comfortable with this than are my American friends. The Europeans do not moralize about this, but instead get right into the spirit of the adventure, whether they are French, German, English, etc. Americans tend to be nervous and uncomfortable. The fact that we have activities that are far more vulgar—lap-dancing, strippers, etc.—to which we take our customers in the States with regularity does not occur to them. Or perhaps it is the exotic nature of the Asian karaoke experience that seems to bother them: the almond-eyed beauties in their *qipaos* or *cheongsams*— the style of dress made famous by Suzie Wong, with its high collar offset with the slit along the legs from waist to ankle—seem to scream sensuality, decadence, and the loss of one's soul to the mysterious East. One almost expects the opium pipes to come out and a lost weekend that ends with sleeping in a ditch along Chang'An Road. All of this is made worse due to the undeniable allure of Asian women for many American and European men, a situation that has led to the depressing state of prostitution in Thailand, Cambodia, the Philippines, and elsewhere. The women who work the karaoke clubs of Beijing and Shanghai—among others—are usually from the country-side, just as they are in Thailand. They come from urban and rural areas in Szechuan Province, for instance, and are prized for their delicate, ivory complexions (the result of the heavy fog that descends upon cities like Chengdu or Chongqing, blotting out the sun) or from farming commu-nities in even more remote provinces. Some come from the north provinces, the ones that border Korea and Russia, and tend to be taller with more voluptuous figures result-ing from the mixing of the races in that part of the world. Or so the stories go.

Should you be doing business in Hong Kong, however, or Shenzhen (the powerhouse industrial and commercial center in Guangdong Province that borders Hong Kong) you may find yourself in Macau. And that's a different story. There, prostitution is decriminalized. The casinos have what are in effect brothels attached to them, and the women come from all over China and the world. You will be as likely to find Russian women and Vietnamese women there as Chinese ladies staying in Macau on a thirty-day pass to make some money for college or to send home to their parents. Some simply rotate between Hong Kong and Macau until immigration gets wise and forbids them entry. Others wind up in different overseas "post-ings" after their stint in Macau, selling sex in Southeast Asia, the Middle East, South America, and even Europe and the States.

Hong Kong itself is no stranger to prostitution and karaoke bars, but it is self-consciously a tourist mecca and for that reason no knowledgeable Chinese or ex-pat would dream of frequenting the overpriced clubs there unless they had literally thousands of US dollars to burn, know-ing they would have little to show for all that flash and cash at the end of the evening. Instead, most will take the jetfoil to Macau: an hour's journey that ends in the casino and the brothel, and an hour's journey back. The whole evening may take no more than five hours total, so you will still be back in your hotel in Hong Kong before midnight, getting a good night's rest before the next round of meetings tomorrow. There are even "travel agencies" at the ferry to Macau that will sell you all-inclusive packages: round-trip ferry, private room, alcohol. The lady you select will usually be compensated separately, however, and is usually not part of the package price, but the private room she takes you to will be covered.

Costs

Of course, costs change too quickly for me to offer anything more than broad guidelines here. We can say with some confidence, however, that the cost of entertaining in China is considerably less expensive than it would be in Europe or the United States. The cost of dining is relatively low at the time of this writing (2007), perhaps two hundred or three hundred dollars for a banquet for fifteen or twenty people if you are in a factory town and outside the major metropolitan centers. The cost goes up in Beijing or Shanghai and may wind up double that amount, depending on the establishment. The cost of "karaoke" will probably be more than your dining costs, but even then my biggest bill came in Beijing at a relatively exclusive club and it was in the neighborhood of US $900 for the evening, involving about five guests, and that was in 2002. Costs have risen in Beijing considerably since then, but are still below what one would reasonably expect to pay in the West. Leave the arrangements to your local contact, making clear your budgetary concerns, and you will be pleased with the results both economically and in terms of your customers' happiness. Of course, I am aiming these remarks at businesspersons working for SMEs and not the Fortune 500 firms that have been spending money lavishly in China, trying to attract and keep important customers. What they do not realize, however, is that the direct, personal approach works far better than throwing money around. If you can build good interpersonal relationships with your clients, they will be satisfied with— even prefer—more casual meals in less-ostentatious surroundings as long as the friendship flows as freely as the *mao tai.*

The second stratagem is to understand your role in China as a foreigner, and to understand what you will be up against: a view of foreigners as decadent, or evil, or colonialists, imperialists, etc. You have to prove yourself to every Chinese you meet, which is exhausting, but there is really no other way open to you particularly if you represent a smaller company with less profile than, say, General Motors. The Chinese are not above exploiting what they can from foreign sources, and you can work that to your advantage if you follow the guidelines described above and adopt Chinese business etiquette. Reading a little about China's history will help you understand some of the mind-set, but you must include in your studies the Mao period because most of your customers grew up during Mao's reign and, indeed, the Communist Party he led is still in control of the country.

Thus, we follow Mao's adage, quoted above: make what is old (courtly etiquette, Maoist philosophy, even prostitution) serve the new (the "New China" business environment), and what is foreign (you and your company) serve China!

Welcome to the Middle Kingdom.

Chapter 3
The Third Stratagem

Use the villages to encircle the city.
                                    —Chairman Mao

The lure of China trade is addictive, and like most addictive drugs it will slowly destroy your nervous system if you're not careful. There is no shame in wanting to penetrate the world's single largest market (in terms of population); the shame comes when you keep trying to succeed in China but fail miserably every time, wasting your company's resources and trying everyone's patience even as you return from every trip with a suitcase full of exotic souvenirs and a head full of amusing anecdotes to share with your colleagues. But no contracts.

One of the most common mistakes people make when it comes to approaching China is to allow themselves to be seduced by the size of the market. Remember that 1.2 billion Chinese do not have the purchasing power of even 300 million Americans. Not yet. The bulk of the Chinese population survives on much less than what we would consider the poverty line in the States. Still, if only ten percent of 1.2 billion people wanted to buy iPods that's one hundred and twenty million iPods. If only one percent of the total Chinese population wanted—and could afford—iPods that's twelve million iPods. Not too shoddy.

But your company does not necessarily manufacture consumer goods. You may be a technology firm, an engineering firm, or a manufacturer of specialty products for a specific industry. That's when you have to approach China more soberly.

I'll give you an example.

One of my businesses involved the manufacture of components for the computer networking industry. These were molded plastic parts, some of which contained copper wiring for use in telephone jacks and for local area networks (LANs), which were used to support voice and data applications. Most of you don't realize this, but if you look around your home and office you will see a plastic faceplate in the wall next to your landline telephone. Your phone is connected with a cable to a jack on this faceplate. If you are working with a computer LAN, then your computer has a cable running from the back of it to another jack, which itself is wired to the routers and servers that are the backbone of your network. Well, the cable, the faceplate, the jack, and the stuff behind the wall that you don't see represents a very competitive multibillion dollar industry. Most of the players in this industry are companies you have never heard of, outside of ATT.

ATT had a product line that covered all the bases in this industry, from the plastic faceplates and phone jacks—connectors—to the routers and servers themselves. They marketed this line under several different names and subsidiaries, from their own ATT Systemax brand and then under Lucent and Avaya incarnations. They were the first big American company to penetrate the Chinese networking market and, as ATT, they were already world-famous so the market was theirs.

Naturally, they dominated in the big cities like Beijing, Shanghai, Hong Kong, and Guangzhou. Other players, such as Siemons, Panduit, Leviton, AMP, and Mod-Tap (all much smaller American firms), were trying desperately to snag whatever crumbs ATT had left behind. Although I had been successful in the Chinese networking market already with the Connecticut-based firm Ortronics,

I was now working for another, even smaller firm with fewer resources and a lot of internal politics working steadily against me and my China campaign.

Oh, yes. This can happen to you. There is a lot of glamour associated with international trade: the long flights to exotic locales, the strange food, foreign languages, and tall tales that you bring back to amaze and annoy your co-workers; and the budget for international travel and expenses, which some of your colleagues want to appropriate for their own departments. You should be aware that the jealousy of your co-workers can be poisonous and can ruin a perfectly good business plan. It's the kind of thing they don't warn you about in Harvard Business School.

So . . . how was I going to introduce yet another player into the already overheated Chinese connector market? It was Peter Wong who quoted Mao to me: use the villages to encircle the city.

Had I made a frontal assault on the heavily fortified Beijing market, for example, I would have spent a small fortune and gotten nowhere. Everyone and his brother considered themselves a China expert, and everyone of these sadly misguided souls was running around the streets and *hutongs* of China's capitol city boasting of their prowess. Each one had their pet customer, whether it was the Beijing Phone Company, China Telecom, China Unicom, or any of a host of other service providers, construction companies, and computer firms. After all, if you are going to spend any amount of time in China you want to be sure it's in one of its biggest cities so that you can satisfy your cheeseburger jones at any time of the day or night. It's a lot tougher to work in the countryside; ask a generation of Chinese intellectuals who were sent there to do hard labor during the Cultural Revolution.

Use the Villages to Encircle the City

Of course. We would concentrate on the smaller companies and the correspondingly smaller orders in the countryside. We would woo the regional phone companies and construction firms. We would conduct seminars in small towns, some with unreliable electric power, so that brownouts and blackouts during our PowerPoint presentations were the norm. (Always have pre-printed versions of your presentation available for just this eventuality.) We would bond with local factory owners, small businessmen and women, and eat in shabby cafés on muddy streets.

Slowly, we built up a presence in the small towns (a small town in China can be the size of Toledo). At the same time, we took out full-page advertising in the trade journals, even though we had no real presence in Beijing or Shanghai other than a small office in the former and a sales rep in the latter. When the smaller companies in the rural areas read the trades and saw our ads, they were mollified. They knew that we had a presence in the market. They started talking to us, and eventually we booked orders.

When you have a resume built up of dozens of small projects throughout China, you appear to be larger and more professional than a company that has a few (admittedly huge) projects in the big cities. Your reliability is not questioned, because of the sheer number of your (admittedly smaller) projects scattered around a large swathe of the Chinese countryside. You have a larger number of companies and persons who can vouch for your competence and the value of your products and services, rather than one guy running the IT department of a large bank or telecomms firm. Don't get me wrong: it's nice to have the big projects because that buys you a lot of "face" in the market; however, you should also realize that the cost of the big projects far outweighs their profit. Yes, that's right: winning the big project could be the worst mistake you can make.

Big Projects versus Small Profits

In the first place, there will always be cost overruns, as every corporate manager knows. In China those overruns can be severe, especially if you lack local expertise. How many local workers will you have to hire to finish the job? What arrangements have to be made for them? How many hours can they be expected to work? What days off will they be entitled to? What about medical expenses for injuries sustained on the job, etc., etc.? You have a hard enough time calculating these things in your own country; in China, it's virtually impossible to estimate all of this in advance with any degree of certainty because the Chinese business environment is not transparent.

What performance benchmarks are part of your contract? Quite often, for a big project, you will be expected to finish certain tasks by a certain date, other tasks by a later date, etc. As we all know, this kind of timeline is subject to all sorts of slings and arrows. In China, there will be meetings that take place on or just after these dates to make sure you are complying with the letter of the contract, rather than its spirit. You may find yourself facing financial penalties if you are not in compliance.

Then, there is the question of local competence. You will quite probably find yourself having to fly in some experts from your own country in order to oversee the project and get it done on time. Their per diem is outrageous, but you will have no choice.

Further, you will be wining and dining the customers on a regular basis if for no other reason than to keep the number of complaints and charges of noncompliance as low as possible. This also will cost you.

Add this to the fact that, in order to win the contract, you quoted a low figure in the first place and you have at least a ten percent holdback that you may never see, and now you are facing potential ruin over this very successful, very high-profile project. You began by drinking champagne to celebrate your victory; you end by crying in your beer.

Thus, what you really need are other—profitable—projects to help offset the possible disaster of the big project. In fact, wasn't that the reason you fought so hard for this big project in the first place so it would help you gain market share? Therefore, take a page from Mao.

Build up your base among the proletariat in the country-side: they will help sustain you during your Long March to victory.

Your Strategic Advantage

You are a newcomer to China. You represent a small firm with big ideas. You know your market well, understand your product offering and its strengths and weaknesses. You have a limited budget, and a lot of people waiting for you to fall on your face (not all of them your competitors). What do you do?

You can't fight a pitched battle; you don't have the troops or the ammunition. So you have to start the way Mao started: as a guerrilla fighter, harassing the enemy's rear. As a small company, you actually have some advantages over your larger competitors. You can fight a hit-and-run campaign. You can show up in one town today, and in another tomorrow. You can move fast and recover from adversity more quickly because you have spent a lot less money. You can build relationships among lower-echelon persons, relationships that will bear fruit later. Your competitors will never know in advance where you will be, or what jobs you are quoting . . . until it's too late. And, best of all, you can change your marketing strategy on a dime.

You can also subcontract a lot of work locally that the big firms can't or won't do. You can print brochures locally, and engage the services of a small—but effective—advertising or marketing firm in China, designing ads and other print media on the fly without waiting for a series of interdepartmental approvals. You can hold press conferences and interviews at the drop of a hat, wherever you happen to be that day. And, to maximize your presence, you can hold business lunches that are free to your potential customers and which are preceded by your sales and marketing pitch. The important thing to remember is that your competitors have a rear to defend; you don't. As a guerrilla fighter, you are constantly on the move, parrying and thrusting, getting the lay of the land, building relationships on the ground. Your competitors can't take anything away from you, but they can lose a lot if you are relentless in your hit-and-run tactics.

Your approach to your customers reflects this strategy. They will ask why they should buy from you and not from your bigger, better-known competitor. The answers you give them are the same as the reasons I am giving you: you are more flexible, more responsive, have lower costs and thus your sales prices are more competitive, you are closer to the local environment, and you can make decisions quickly. You don't have a board of directors or a bunch of shareholders to impress. You won't nickel and dime your customers to death. You don't have impossible legal boilerplate to insist upon in your distribution or sales representative contracts; your approach to the market conditions are thus more realistic than those of your competitor. You are, in short, the perfect compromise between Western technological expertise and manufacturing on the one hand, and Chinese-style business practices on the other.

And that's your story, and you're sticking to it.

We will discuss the structure of your "guerrilla band" in more detail in Chapter Five. For now, it is useful to know that the smaller your core sales and marketing group, the easier your life will be in the first year or so of business in China. While your home office will be expected to provide support in terms of engineering and technical issues, your China team should be small, carefully selected, and highly motivated. The hours will be long, travel arduous, and there will be a constant demand for creative thinking and problem solving. In addition, there will be a requirement for constant updates and reports from your home office, which will drive you (and your team) to distraction.

The team should be composed of all local talent; the only non-Chinese national will be you, and you will provide guidance for the China team and simultaneously serve as liaison to your home office. This will be a very demanding, very stressful position at first and you should be in good physical (and mental) health. In addition, you need to have your supply lines established and secure: this means that a financing pipeline needs to be in place. Although this sounds like common sense, you would be surprised how many problems arise when a small company attempts to navigate the complexities of international banking, wire transfers, etc.

It will be less expensive in the long run if you are stationed in China for several months at a time, rather than flying back and forth from Europe or the States. You will not be able to put your strategies or a coherent sales and marketing campaign into place long-distance. There is a Chinese proverb that says "a long sleep has many dreams": i.e., if you do not maintain a constant presence—not only in the market, but with your local team—you will lose your customers and your team as they seek other options. You can't expect that your sales force will maintain a decent level of commitment if you are not there.

When you apply the strategy using villages to encircle the city, you need to be present in those villages. A long-distance relationship is much harder to maintain in the villages, because your customers there are already irritated by the way the bureaucrats in the capitol remain aloof from their problems and concerns. You, as a foreigner, are even more remote—not only in terms of physical distance but in terms of culture—so you must try to reduce the distance as much as possible. Even though you will have a local team in place to handle the day-to-day, your own presence (as often and as consistently as possible) is absolutely necessary in order to raise the comfort level in your customers. So many foreign firms have cut and run after the first year or so in China that the customer base is leery of embracing another. Thus, your obstacles include those that have been set up by other foreign companies you've never even heard of, and which are long gone. Sad, but true.

Imagine Mao and his band of rebels. They need to establish support among the people in the countryside, and they can't do that by passing through town and handing out brochures. They need to demonstrate their concern for the villages, their knowledge of the special problems each villager faces, the type of infrastructure to be found there, and the range of possible solutions. The forces arrayed against Mao were better-equipped and formally trained; they had nicer uniforms, and represented the war lords who were already authority figures. Mao had to propose an attractive and viable alternative to the war lords; he had to empower the people themselves.

This is not your typical American or European approach to marketing. For one thing, it's too much trouble: it requires specialized knowledge of the environment, the time necessary to cultivate good personal relationships, and a marketing campaign that is flexible and tailor-made to each situation. For a Fortune 500 company, the cost would be prohibitive. They can print thousands of brochures and place hundreds of full-page, four-color ads in the local trades, but the kind of one-on-one relationship we are discussing is usually out of their range. For one thing, it would require a different marketing strategy for each "village," and that is not what they teach you in B-school.

You, however, *are* the marketing strategy. You can develop a different set of options for each condition you face. Of course, you may have a generalized approach that is characteristic of the company you work for; that is what your corporate profile is made of, and your corporate image. However, on the ground, this needs a lot of tweaking to make it work in a region as vast and as deep as China.

Why? Isn't China a homogenous country where everyone speaks the same language, shares the same history and culture, and has the same expectations? You may be of an age to remember those newsreels of hundreds of thousands of Chinese in Tian An Men Square during the Cultural Revolution in the 1960s and 1970s, dressed in identical Mao jackets and waving their identical copies of the *Little Red Book*, and you came away with the impression that "they were all alike."

(Buzzer sound.) Wrong! Thank you for playing! Next contestant!

In order to use the villages to encircle the city, we better visit those villages and find out who lives there.

What Villages?

Where are the villages? A number of books have been published in recent years that attempt to show the reader where the action is outside of Beijing. They identify specific regions—such as Jilin or Chengdu—and analyze their importance for trade and the possibility of doing business there. The information is all well and good, for now (things change quickly in China), but is of little use to a small or medium-sized enterprise such as your own. You don't have the luxury of picking and choosing where you will go because you don't have the time, money, or other resources to invest in a long-term strategy similar to those of a Fortune 500. What has probably happened is that you have received a request from a sales agent or maybe even a factory in China, and now you are contemplating what to do, studying that email or letter like a shaman poring over entrails. Alternatively, you have been told by so many friends and colleagues how great the market in China can be that you are now considering your first trip and don't know where to start. "I'm going to China," you tell yourself.

Really? Where, Exactly?

In the first place, there is no such country as "China." Get used to that idea right away. To prove this point, all you have to do is pick up any history of "China" covering the past, say, three or four thousand years and go through the maps. You don't even have to read the book, just look at the maps and watch how what was "China" one day was replaced by an entirely different "China" on another day. Sometimes there were even two or more "Chinas" at the same time. What we call "China" is actually a kind of confederation of different nationalities, different cultures, and different languages, all ruled by the iron hand of the Communist Party. By accepting today's definition of "China"—the definition as provided by the government of the "People's Republic of China"—one collaborates in a kind of fiction (one that includes Tibet, for instance). China is not a country in any kind of Western sense of the word; rather, "China" is *virtual reality*.

Do you know someone who speaks Chinese? Actually, you don't. There is no such thing as the "Chinese" language, just as there is no such thing as the "European" language. There is the Chinese character set, that collection of more than 40,000 hieroglyphs that comprise a written language, but it can be used to write anything: from Japanese to Korean to Vietnamese . . . to English.

What we call "Chinese" is actually any one of dozens of languages and thousands of dialects spoken in that Asian landmass our maps identify as "China." If someone speaks Mandarin, for instance, they will not be understood by someone who speaks only Cantonese. Phonetically, there is as much similarity between Mandarin and Cantonese as exists between, say, Italian and Spanish or between French and Romanian. You may be able to tease out a word here or there that sounds familiar, but you won't be able to understand a complete sentence.

Thus, when I was studying "Chinese" in New York City in the 1970s I could not understand what the Chinese in Chinatown were saying because they were speaking either Cantonese or Hokkien or some other, southern, language while I was studying Mandarin, the "official" language of "China," which at that time was rarely spoken outside of either China or Taiwan, where Mandarin was the official, government-mandated language. Of course, the shop owners and restauranteurs in Chinatown wrote their signs and menus in Chinese characters which made communication a little easier . . . except that they did not use the simplified characters created by the government in Beijing but the more complicated old characters that are still in use by the government in Taipei and in the Chinese diaspora generally.

(The above is useful information, by the way. When you design a brochure to be used in China you must ensure that the character set being used is the one used in China and not in the Chinese diaspora, which uses the old characters. It's not that the Chinese will not understand the old characters—many will—but it is a signal that you are consulting overseas Chinese and possibly Taiwanese; this could be insulting or in some other way cause some discomfort if not paranoia. Also, the Chinese are very proud of their modernizations of the character set and would tend to look down upon anyone who does not use it as a country bumpkin. You don't need this kind of aggravation, so it just makes life easier if your brochures and other printed materials reflect the modern, simplified character set.)

I am not trying to be picky here. There is a method to my mad insistence that there is no such place as "China" and no such language as "Chinese." It forces you to understand that any attempt at generalizing where China is concerned is doomed to failure, and this failure will be hard-wired into any marketing strategy you employ. While I do not suggest, nor recommend, that you learn Mandarin *and* Cantonese *and* Shanghainese *and* Hokkien, etc.—Mandarin will be useful for most general purposes thanks to the stern measures undertaken by the government in Beijing to suppress anything else—I do recommend that you understand the cultural and linguistic differences that exist between different groups of "Chinese" people, particularly as you employ the "use the villages" approach, which is directed at the differences between the ethnic communities rather than their similarities.

In order to institutionalize their grip on the far-flung provinces of their country, the government in Beijing did two very important things which they copied from their Soviet counterparts: they made one language—the language of the capitol—the official language of the whole country and did what they could to stamp out rival tongues; and they moved people around, especially those in positions of authority, so you had Mandarin-speaking bureaucrats taking over in Cantonese-speaking areas, for instance. When it came to Tibet, the result was even more extreme, so that now Tibet is run and populated largely by Han Chinese and not by Tibetans. The same is true in Xinjiang Province in the extreme west of China, where the ruling elite is Han Chinese but the local people are largely Uzbeks, Uighurs, Tajiks, and other Caucasians who claim Islam as their religion.

As a sales person, your goal is to cement relationships on the ground with the people who matter to your business. Thus, in China, the first phase of this approach involves understanding the Han Chinese who control the country. They are the ones who call the shots in the major utilities, the construction companies, and the technology companies. They will be able to make or break you. They speak Mandarin—either as their native language or as the one they use for government and business—and their history books have pictures of Mao in them.

However, you must also be sensitive to the other nationalities of China, for the simple reason that the free-market economy is creating a new class of decision-makers in virtually every province. This new breed of Chinese businessperson may be Shanghainese or Cantonese or even Uzbek or Tibetan. The Chinese Communist Party will do what it can to control the growth and power of the non-Han people, especially in the markets, but that does not mean it will be successful. When the Chinese government loosened up their economic controls and de-nationalized their factories and businesses, they let the running dogs out. In my business dealings in China over the past ten years alone, I have dealt with Manchurians and Mongolians, as well as Uzbeks and Tajiks. I've been invited to the Gobi Desert on horseback to camp out under the stars and drink Mongolian beer until we can hear the voice of the Khan as it sails over the singing sands; I've haggled in the marketplaces of Urumqi over captured (or stolen?) Soviet binoculars and fatigue caps. I've eaten meals of *halal* lamb boiled in a spicy broth in Beijing, courtesy of my Chinese Muslim customers, while we traded quotations from the *Qur'an*.

And I've eaten huge banquets in Beijing where never a grain of rice was to be found, because the northerners like their wheat and their bread and their noodles, thus shattering the stereotype we have in the West of Chinese people obsessed with their rice bowls.

When you go to the villages then this is what you will find: a different China from the one you grew up thinking you knew. A vast China. A China that is only a convenient term covering a wealth of cultures, languages, cuisines, and attitudes, in an ongoing yet uneasy relationship with each other. It is probably safe to say that almost all citizens of China are proud of their country and its accomplishments over the past sixty years since the success of the Revolution, and that this pride in China's recent past is mixed with their identification with China's more ancient history and culture. But there is also regional pride and identification, and this includes the citizens' own language and customs. China has not yet become perfectly homogenized, as much as the bureaucrats would like to think so. The massive movement of populations that has taken place across China by government fiat has succeeded in reducing some of the regional chauvinism, but not all. When I was in Beijing several years ago, there were bus bombings in the streets carried out—it was said—by ethnic Uighurs protesting their treatment by the government in far off Xinjiang Province.

How Green is My Guanxi

You will not become embroiled in these conflicts, obviously, but you need to be aware of them. They can work in your favor. In the provinces far from the traditional seats of power—economic and political—you will find a rather more integrated economy with interlocking spheres of influence. If you are successful in negotiating a contract for some telephone systems in, for instance, remote Gansu Province you will find yourself in a good position to win other contracts in Gansu Province that have nothing to do with your first customer . . . for the simple fact that the person who bought your system at the phone company has a brother who runs a construction firm; that brother needs some wiring for his projects, and in turn will introduce you to his son-in-law who is working for the local government office, and so on. This is known as *guanxi*—connections—and you have probably heard this term used before by people who have already been to China or you've read it in the books about Chinese business you can find in most bookstores. *Guanxi* is no laughing matter; it is a vitally important marketing tool, not only in China but everywhere in Asia and, indeed, the world. It is just more ubiquitous in China, a fact of life in an economy that for decades was run by a Central Committee, which means it was not really running well at all. A factory that produced cars, for instance, had a constant need for rubber for tires and hose; they did not produce rubber products themselves but had to source them elsewhere. That meant that a requisition had to go from the factory to a central government office that would put the request on a list. If that factory was lucky, they would get the rubber they needed sometime that year.

In order to make the factory reach its production quotas on time, the factory director had to become creative. He would build personal relationships with the directors of other factories, factories that produced the components or the raw materials that he needed for his own production. That was *guanxi*. The factory director would still put in his request for the needed goods through proper channels, but they would be drop-shipped to him immediately from his pals at the other factories. When eventually they received the official requirement from the government office, the goods had already been shipped and the request fulfilled . . . which made *them* look efficient, too.

As China moved into a market economy, these connections were still important and, in fact, even more so. With everyone clamoring for goods and services, you needed your own personal connections to stay on top of the situation and stay supplied. Further, once the government got out of the commercial side of the economy and de-controlled the factories, the factories had to make a profit for the first time since the Revolution. They needed to make sales, and for this, *guanxi* was vitally necessary. With *guanxi* you knew who was in the market for your goods and, even more important, if they had the hard currency to afford them. And with *guanxi* you could virtually assure that you would get the sale and not your competitor, provided your *guanxi* was better than his.

The term became so overused and abused that it became a matter of some levity at the trade shows in Beijing and elsewhere in China: "Do you have *guanxi*?" "Sure, do you have *guanxi*?" "Oh, yeah. How good is yours?" "Great! I have great *guanxi*."

In the "villages," *guanxi* is just as important as it is in the city. In fact, that scruffy looking midlevel engineer at the Number Five Silicone Carbide Rod Manufacturing Facility in Zibo City, Shandong Province, has an old college buddy who is now in charge of the Number Two Rayon Manufacturing Facility in Baoding, Hebei Province. Between the two of them, they could provide you with more than ten million dollars worth of trade in electrical frequency converters. You would never have heard of the requirement in Baoding had it not been for your careful cultivation of the engineer in Zibo. Chinese firms don't actually post their RFQs (Request for Quotation) in the newspapers. Many of these wish lists are word-of-mouth or, at the very least, they have been decided long before the requisition has been officially advertised.

So . . . how do you reward the engineer in Zibo City? After all, he did you a favor and introduced you to another potential project and a reliable customer. Do you hand him a couple hundred dollars and say "Thanks"?

What do you think?

La Mordida

Corruption is as illegal in China as it is in the United States. Worse, if you are caught bribing people in China—or in any other country—you can be indicted in your own country, depending on its laws concerning corruption. If you are a US citizen, you can be arrested, tried, and convicted of corruption even if the corruption took place overseas.

So, how to deal with this issue?

The problem of corruption, bribery, and simple "compensation" comes in this chapter because it is as commonplace in the villages as in the cities, but in the cities the process is more sophisticated due to the ever-present watchful eye of the Party and the Public Security Bureau over high-profile transactions, particularly those involving foreigners.

In the first place, what we call a bribe in the West is a moveable feast. In the US government, for instance, every time someone wants to pass a bill for something we can all agree upon—more money for education, for instance, or a much-needed bridge or highway—there are attachments for "pork": an appropriate metaphor, by they way, considering the present context of China trade. These attachments or riders to the bill are often for millions of dollars worth of projects that have nothing to do with the main bill, but when they are included they ensure the support of other senators or representatives who will benefit by these allocations. We are too fussy to call those bribes, but that is what they are. What else should we call them? Salaries?

The same thing happens all over the world, but in different manifestations. In Mexico, a bribe is called "*la mordida*," the "bite," and is an added cost of doing almost anything. You can avoid a traffic ticket by giving a *mordida* to the cop who pulled you over; you pretty much have to, or else spend the night (or longer) in a Mexican jail while the miserable cop fills out the paperwork. Mexican police are notoriously underpaid, so the bribe is part of their livelihood.

In China, especially now when there is no more job security—no more "iron rice bowl" as it was known in the days before Deng Xiao Ping said "to get rich is glorious"—people more than ever need to find additional funds, not only to survive but to send their children to good schools or to buy a much-needed refrigerator or fan. The farmers in the countryside used to be the wealthy cousins: they were permitted to sell whatever they grew over and above the quota demanded by the government. That resulted in Chinese farmers being able to buy automobiles and go on trips abroad, while their poorer cousins in the cities—who had no way of earning additional money—seethed in anger and jealousy, riding their bicycles for two hours or more every day to work, in every kind of weather, just to make the equivalent of one hundred dollars a month or less. If you think the Tian An Men Square demonstrations of 1989 were about democracy alone, think again. The economy was at the heart of the protest, with college students in Beijing and Shanghai and other major cities facing the grim reality that tuition costs and living costs were rising while the earning power of their parents was not. The villages were truly encircling the cities.

Now, the situation has changed considerably. The money is being made by companies, some of them brand new, in the cities; but competition in China is as fierce as it is anywhere and this has led to massive corruption and several very high-profile cases. The most famous of these involves the former mayor of Shanghai, the legendary Chen Liangyu.

A Case in Point

In the autumn of 2006, Mr. Chen was relieved of his position as Party Secretary in the Shanghai government and taken to an undisclosed location. The charge was corruption, on a scale that was large even by Chinese standards. It is, however, a useful guide to the twin concepts of *guanxi* and corruption.

Mr. Chen—educated as an architect in Great Britain—was one of the most influential political and economic leaders Shanghai (and China) had ever known. He turned Shanghai into the powerhouse economic center that it is today, and this was at the behest of the Chinese Communist Party. The idea was to replace Hong Kong as

China's economic capitol, especially with regard to foreign investment and trade. The "one country, two systems" approach that China took to the former British colony when it was returned to them in 1997 will not last forever. Instead, China wanted to expand Shanghai's allure for foreign investment capital, and Chen Liangyu was the man for the job.

He changed Shanghai's skyline in a matter of years. From the surreal landscape of Pudong—with its miles of skyscrapers, each one a different style and even a different color—to Tomorrow Square, the $300 million tennis stadium and the $1 billion Formula One racetrack, Shanghai has become a world-class city. This was accomplished by using public funds to finance private projects, privatization of public utilities, and eventually led to Mr. Chen controlling more than forty percent of "Shanghai, Inc," an industry that includes everything from Shanghai's banks to its construction companies and factories. Although the others arrested with Mr. Chen included his brother-in-law and even his own son, there are Party officials aplenty in prison along with him. It will probably take years to unravel and disentangle the complex web of deals, bribes, banking irregularities, and "*guanxi*" that formed the core of Shanghai, Inc., but what we can take away from this episode is the simple fact that business in China is run this way. Family members, Party officials, college roommates, former co-workers, everyone forms part of this network of relationships that can prove to be rewarding and enriching in more than just the social sense. No Chinese is an island; every person you meet maintains some degree of *guanxi* in their lives, or they would not survive: not in a cultural or social sense, but also not in an economic sense. They may not even understand or describe their relationships as *guanxi*, except when they can exploit a relationship for some tangible benefit.

In Mr. Chen's case, he would not have become the famous, populist leader he was in Shanghai's government had it not been for his *guanxi*: his close relationship with a future President of China, Jiang Zemin. It was Jiang who was instrumental in crafting Shanghai's new persona as a magnet for foreign investment, and when he became President he nominated a number of old Shanghai friends to important posts in the new government. One of these was Mr. Chen.

In many ways, New China is a reflection of a Shanghainese approach to modernity, sophistication, and a sense of cosmopolitan *nobless oblige*. Shanghai had always been China's "New York City," and with the end of Mao and the beginning of a number of economic reforms Shanghai found itself front and center, representing the new thought and new consciousness that has attracted so many foreign businesses, tourists, and political insiders to a city that has long had a reputation as being open to the outside world.

Along with all that cash and flash, however, was a dark side. As China's putative financial center and draw for foreign investment and foreign currency, the amount of money that could be made there dazzled many an entrepreneur. Soon, it was not only the higher-level executives who had their hands out for a nice fat envelope, it was middle-level managers and Party officials, as well. The Party—I stress once again—still controls China. As soon as any project gets big enough, there will be a Party official somewhere on the board, watching to make sure that the transactions reflect Marxism, Leninism, and Mao Ze Dong thought. However, Party officials, too, are human (much to everyone's disbelief) and they can be bribed, and are. In the case of Shanghai, Inc. and Chen Liangyu, there were a number of Party officials on the take.

The "Party line" on the Chen story is that there was so much bribery and corruption that he had to be shut down. The real story is certainly somewhat different, and it may never be known. It is possible that there were those in the Beijing government who were jealous of Chen and his amazing successes in Shanghai; it is possible that Mr. Chen was a little too arrogant in his power and was not worshipful enough at the feet of the Party. The Party, after all, is your "mother and father" according to one old Communist-era song, and honoring one's parents is a trademark of Confucian practice. Tracing the Chen story, however, is an excellent exercise for those of you curious about just how *guanxi* works, for it involved every industry of any size or merit in Shanghai and the money that changed hands can be computed in the hundreds of millions of dollars.

Which brings us to you.

Don't Ask, Don't Tell

You are not Mr. Chen. (Thankfully, perhaps, or you would now be in a Chinese prison. China executes those convicted of bribery, and an arrest in China is a conviction.) Instead, you are a small, foreign businessman who is just trying to succeed in China trade. You are forbidden by law—both China's and your own country's—from becoming involved in corruption and bribery. If you are caught, the ramifications would be dire and could include execution in China (though that has happened rarely when foreigners are involved; usually they may be deported after some months or years in a Chinese prison). And, anyway, you have no idea whom to bribe, or how, or how much, even if you wanted to. Which you don't. And yet, here I am telling you that bribery greases the wheels of industry in China.

The solution is simple. I promised to tell you the truth about doing business in China, and this is one issue that has to be addressed. It's not a solution I am recommending, mind you, and after all, not every job in China involves corruption and bribery. You can probably manage quite well without "rewarding" helpful behavior, as long as your competitors are equally squeaky clean. And as long as their sales agents and sales reps are clean. And their local staff.

The sad but inevitable solution is: leave any questions of corrupt practices and bribery up to your local people. You don't want to get involved. You don't want to know what's going on. You don't want to discuss it, even. As far as you are concerned, you and your company and its agents and representatives are not involved in anything remotely connected to bribery or corruption. I mean, who knows what your sales agent did with that ten percent commission you paid him on the last job, right? That's got nothing to do with you. If he paid some of that money to someone on the inside to get a job, you will never know, and believe me you don't want to know.

Chinese agents understand the difficulty Americans and other Westerners get into when it comes to these issues and will keep you removed from this activity. So, my advice is to pursue a "don't ask, don't tell" policy in China. You will get into considerable legal trouble if you get involved, so don't.

Just understand that this does not mean that bribery is not taking place right under your nose. That's just the way we do things in the villages.

Chapter 4
The Fourth Stratagem

Guerrilla strategy must be based primarily on alertness, mobility, and attack. It must be adjusted to the enemy situation, the terrain, the existing lines of communication, the relative strengths, the weather and the situation of the people.

—Chairman Mao

As hinted in the previous chapter, your strategy as an SME in China must be based on your strengths which another, larger company would consider your weaknesses: small size, ability to change direction quickly, ability to make decisions on the fly. Your lack of funds means you have to think smarter and work smarter rather than take the "human wave" approach of your competitors.

Your competitors, by the way, have been reading the other business books: the ones that tell you how to interpret the writings of Lao Tzu or Sun Tzu in terms of business practices. While these are certainly venerable Chinese sages with a wealth of worldly—and other-worldly—wisdom at their fingertips, the suggestions given in the business texts are usually more useful for those in larger, more affluent firms and, besides, when was the last time someone in Mao's China actually read Lao Tzu?

This chapter will be devoted to some anecdotes that will reveal by example the kind of strategies I believe will work for you as they have worked for me and the companies I represented for more than twenty years in China trade.

Saturday Night in Baoding

There was a fascinating and moving book with the above title written by Richard Terrill and published by the University of Arkansas Press in 1990. What is noteworthy about the book first of all is that it takes place in Baoding, Hebei Province, which is where I signed my first contracts in China. In fact, I would have been arriving in Baoding just as Mr Terrill was leaving, in 1986.

I had already been involved in Chinese contract nego-tiations, as early as 1984, when I proposed some sophisti-cated computer systems based on the Digital Equipment Corporation's new VAX machines, but those negotiations took place in New York City. Later, I would wind up in China overseeing the installation of the systems and train-ing the operators.

But in 1986, we were in Baoding, a place I had never heard of until I started working for Anthony Chang. We flew from Hong Kong to Beijing, had a quick lunch, and then started on a grueling drive in a rattling van south to the Baoding Guest House (*Baoding Bing Guan*) and had dinner that night with the Mayor of Baoding, a man who reminded me of the actor Victor Mature.

It is hard to communicate the enormity of the experi-ence to those who have only been to China's big cities and then only recently. In 1986, I was one of the few foreigners most Baodingers had ever seen. I literally stopped traffic when I walked down a street. When I entered a restaurant, all conversation would stop and everyone would stare at me until I disappeared into one of the private rooms with Anthony and our local contacts or customers.

That first night in Baoding, in an outdoor pavilion all old wood and red lacquer under a Chinese moon, along with about a dozen people I did not know yet but who would become influential in my first years in China, we ate dozens of exotic dishes I had never tasted before. In my briefcase was about ten million dollars worth of projects we were quoting on, but no business was discussed that night. For Anthony Chang, going to China was going home and he reveled in the position he had of a sophisticated New Yorker on one side—a successful Western businessman with a home in Greenwich—and one of China's own lost sons on the other, a man whose father had been a successful international businessman from Shandong Province before Mao's Revolution. Anthony's passion was for Beijing Opera, Yentai pears, *jiao-zi* (dumplings) and *bao-zi* (steamed buns) . . . and roast beef sandwiches from Carnegie Deli. He and I had common ground when it came to New York City . . . but in China he was in another element and I had some catching up to do.

There were a number of projects we were quoting on. One was for a high-speed rubber extrusion line, to make seals for cars. Another was for a set of frequency inverters for their rayon factory. Yet another involved a complete factory for making roofing material. And so on.

Baoding was not exactly on the A list where foreign investment was concerned. There were few foreign companies competing there, and those that were were not American but Japanese, German, and Italian: the Axis Powers, so to speak. The irony was not lost on me. Once again, World War II would be fought on Chinese soil.

The only reason we were in Baoding in the first place was *guanxi*: Anthony had connections there, or, to be more specific, his *brother* had connections there.

His brother—and most of the rest of his family—had been left behind in China when the Revolution ended. In 1986, his brother was a senior engineer for one of China's more important ministries in Beijing. He had the connections in Baoding and knew where the money was. Many companies in China will look for proposals and quotations from foreign firms, but not actually have the hard currency to pay for them. It is something of an art to know who actually has the money; once that is known, there are sharks in the water, circling and waiting to strike.

Anthony's brother had that information. Baoding was poised to become a manufacturing center, an important city in Hebei Province. It boasted many factories already; some had to be upgraded to modern technology (the last upgrades had usually been under the Soviets, who were hardly in a position to upgrade themselves much less their Chinese comrades). Others were starting pretty much from scratch. But in the 1980s, China was the Wild West.

Chinese companies had been given the green light by the government to upgrade their facilities. The idea was to turn China into a competitive nation in terms of technology and manufacturing in a single generation. That meant the Chinese had government money at their disposal to acquire much-needed heavy equipment, process controls, electrical equipment, and computer systems from abroad. Until Nixon had opened China for America, the only countries doing business there were the Japanese (whom the Chinese had never really forgiven for the hideous crimes the Japanese perpetrated during their invasion and occupation of that country), and the Germans and Italians. The Soviets were also an important trading partner, but they treated the Chinese like second-class citizens. The Arab countries were also in evidence, but they did not have very much to trade with the Chinese aside from oil and some other natural resources. When it came to brand-name technology, there were only a few players and that included the United States.

It is safe to say that when Anthony and I arrived in Baoding there were no other American competitors in that city. As long as we could sell what the Chinese wanted at a reasonable price, we were in. That meant, however, that I would have to give detailed technical presentations on all of these projects to satisfy the first phase of the negotiation.

Which was fine, except that if you review the above representative list of projects, you'll see that I was expected to know all there was to know about everything, from rubber extrusion to frequency inverters. It usually takes about a lifetime to learn all there is to know about rubber extrusion—an extremely complex operation that involves curing the rubber as it is extruded—and many more years of experience in electronics to convince a buyer that your frequency inverter is the best in the business.

I knew nothing of either one—or any other—of these projects. All I knew is what I had memorized from the technical proposals we were sent by the manufacturers and a few phone calls I had with them before I left. My responsibility, therefore, was daunting. However, I had an ace up my sleeve.

One advantage you will have as a foreigner in China is *not* speaking the language. Going through an interpreter gives you two options, both of which I used relentlessly during every negotiation I have ever had in China: (a) using an interpreter gives you time to collect your thoughts and reassess your position every step of the way, and (b) if you say something that the Chinese obviously feel is wrong, you can always blame it on the essence of your comment being "lost in translation." You simply try again, rephrasing what you are saying and hoping that you have rephrased it enough to give the right answer.

Further, using a translator means that the negotiation will take twice as long as it normally would. That also buys you time, as tricky parts of the technical presentation can be postponed naturally—due to lunch, dinner, etc.—thus giving you time to refresh your memory, recalculate costs, contact your home office for advice, etc. As an SME, you will not be in China with an entire technical team at your disposal, so making the best use of time is critical to your success. If you are fortunate enough to have a tech team with you, however, you will be able to confer with them during the breaks to make sure you don't say anything stupid.

Between the long pauses as I waited for the translations—both of my words into Mandarin, and the Mandarin of my customers into English—I was able to think clearly about what I wanted to say and how deeply I was going to commit my company to a course of action. There was no way to force me into any kind of concessions, because the negotiations simply lacked that kind of momentum.

We worked late into the night, which meant that we had dinner with our customers every evening and quite often this involved (and still involves) a great deal of drinking. Anthony was allergic to alcohol—not unknown among some Chinese—so I was the designated drinker for most of these events. Never a heavy drinker under the best of circumstances back in the States, I suddenly developed this reputation for drinking in China. That meant that the word would spread, and at the next banquet—even in another town—our clients would know how much I drank at the last banquet and therefore try to see if I could beat my previous record!

One has to know one's terrain, as Mao said above, as well as the "situation of the people." In this case, eating out at the company's expense—yours or your client's—is the only entertainment and relief from the monotony of small-town factory life that these men and women have. In small-town China, people are at home in bed by nine or ten o'clock. Dinner usually starts around 6 pm and lasts until 8 or 8:30. One drinks as much as one can during that time, for one never knows when there will be another opportunity. One eats as much as one can, as well. The food served at banquets of this type is usually of greater variety and better quality than the food the locals eat every day, so you will see a rotation taking place if you are negotiating with the same company for more than a day or so, as different people show up for successive banquets: it's just their "turn."

After dinner, it was normal for me to return to my hotel room—the ancient and drafty Baoding Guest House, which was less a hotel in any traditional sense and more of a kind of Bates Motel—and work through the night. This was before laptop computers and printers; everything we did had to be typed (by me) on a portable electric typewriter that we picked up in Hong Kong on our way to China. When we had finalized a certain portion of the technical specifications, I would type them up—pages and pages of them—so that they would be ready for photo-copying at 7 am the next morning. I also sent telexes and received them from our office in the States. For those of you too young to know what a telex is, it's what we used before there were personal computers, the Internet, and email. A telex was, quite simply, a telegram; the difference being that I typed them up myself on long strings of paper tape with holes punched in them and handed them to a telex operator to send. In New York, a telex machine there would start rattling as my telex was received in real time and my message printed out.

I sent dozens of these every night. Often, they were urgent requests for more information, more technical spec-ifications, more clarification on costs and delivery times. Sometimes they were announcements that we had suc-cessfully negotiated another project. We rarely had time to celebrate, however, as we had constant business and a steady flow of courier packages from the States with all-new project information for more technology of which I had no earthly clue.

This was also in the days before cell phones, and much of China at that time had very poor landline serv-ice (still does), so we sometimes had to wait for hours for a connection to the States, and then you had to shout. In fact, getting a phone call to Beijing was just as trouble-some and the connection just as bad. Thus, the "existing lines of communication" were neither. We had to work very hard for every phone call and every telex and every fax, and even harder to put all of this in typed and final form for signatures. A single typographical error on a long contract document could keep me up an additional hour or two at night as I tried to "correct" the error by retyping the page and then making more errors since I was bleary-eyed and exhausted.

The sum total of all this is that I got very little sleep on these trips to the interior. Even our transportation was of questionable quality and efficiency. There were some occa-sions during which we took the train from Beijing to

Baoding rather than the car (which had proved to be a problem because we were not allowed to stop at all on the road, certain areas being off-limits to foreigners), and taking a train in China in 1986 was an adventure itself, and that's being euphemistic. With all of these problems and issues, however, we managed to do quite well and it was a combination of Anthony's *guanxi* and knowledge of the culture and mores of China, with a lot of dedicated and relentless work.

We negotiated for the rubber extrusion line and for the frequency inverters that week, as well as for several other, smaller projects. They all involved machinery from the United States, bought from companies that were not present in China in any other capacity. We acted simply as middle-men, buying the equipment and reselling it to the Chinese through an interlocking system of letters of credit and letters of assignment of proceeds. This meant that we did not have to front any of the money for the machinery or equipment; we simply assigned the down payments to the sellers off of the letters of credit. This is a system that few SMEs were aware of—and few banks, unless they were involved internationally—but which works quite well when you have limited cash flow. When we received the letter of credit as payment from our customers, the letter of assignment of proceeds against the L/C meant that the sellers (or whomever we assigned proceeds to) would receive their funds first, and we would receive the balance. Thus, for a four million dollar rubber hose extrusion line, there might have been a twenty percent down payment (as an example). In this case, that meant eight hundred thousand dollars would be paid to us before we shipped. Out of that eight hundred thousand, the manufacturer of the rubber hose line would be paid first; if we had agreed on a down payment to them of one hundred thousand, then they would receive one hundred thousand at once. We would only receive the balance after they had been paid. In reality, this all takes place at the same time and everyone is happy. There will be another payment when the machinery is shipped, and another payment upon successful installation. And, of course, there will be that ten percent holdback, to be paid at some time in the future.

Thus, as an SME operating in China for the first time, our only real upfront costs were those for airfare, hotels, and meals and entertainment. Even the cost of the equipment we sold was covered by our system of L/Cs and letters of assignment of proceeds against those same L/Cs.

That first year in China we grossed something like six million dollars in Baoding, and we were only three people in a small office near the World Trade Center.

Alertness, Mobility, and Attack

Our great asset in China in the 1980s was Anthony's small but active network, beginning with his brother and the Baoding connection. Once the dust had settled, our small company had grossed more than ten million dollars in that town alone, and that's in 1980s dollars. In 1987 and 1988, we managed to sell more frequency inverters, and a complete line for the manufacture of modified bitumen roofing material (sourced from the Ruemmer Company of Bamberg, Germany) that had the vice-governor of Hebei Province himself show up for the contract signing, which was televised. It was the second-largest contract ever signed in Hebei Province at the time. We had Italian and Japanese competitors for that one, and oddly enough they shared the train carriage with us on our way down to Shijiazhuang—Hebei's capitol—for the final negotiations. They did not realize that we were their competitors, so they spoke freely about the upcoming meetings. Fortunately, I was able to understand some Italian so I learned some valuable tactical information that day. I do not speak Japanese at all, but we knew from our inside sources that they had no chance of getting the job anyway.

Something I learned from working with Anthony Chang was to take nothing for granted, and to never rest on your laurels. If there was money to be made anywhere in China, we were there . . . even if that meant leaving one town in the middle of the night to race across a thousand miles to show up somewhere else the next day for another negotiation. We were only two people—plus our *guanxi*, of course—but we were everywhere. Intelligence was vital to our success, and we were gluttons for it. China is a hotbed of gossip, rumor, and innuendo: one has to learn to separate the wheat from the chaff. There is also a certain amount of deceit that takes place, and one has to be careful about that, too. In one case known to me personally, an executive from another American firm had spent a small fortune in China in the belief that he would be awarded a certain project. As it turned out, he lost that project but was not aware that *it had already been signed by another firm*. He appeared in Beijing and asked his putative customers out to dinner, as usual. They accepted, as usual. They had a great time.

The following day he learned from someone else that they had signed with his competitor weeks before. His rage was so great, he phoned the customers and screamed at them and then left the country.

In another case, I was standing in the airport lounge at Shanghai waiting for my connecting flight to Beijing. A man I had never seen before—an older white American in a business suit and florid complexion, as if on the verge of a nervous breakdown—came straight up to me and demanded, "Are you as sick and tired of this country as I am?"

It turns out he was the head of an electronics manufacturing firm in the States who was negotiating a complex technology transfer deal with the Chinese to make capacitors. The negotiations were typically Chinese: every time you thought you had a deal, you found out you didn't; there was one more thing to be discussed, one more issue to be resolved. He had been back and forth with them over a period of months, and still had no contract. He was fuming, nearly apoplectic. He told me, "I am never eating Chinese food again, never going near a Chinese restaurant! If I see Chinese on the street, I'm crossing the street to avoid them! I can't stand it here anymore!"

I was sympathetic, of course. I knew what he was going through. We had negotiated contracts in sessions that went on for weeks ourselves. I knew the roller coaster ride he was on. But he had made some fundamental mistakes in his approach to the market, and the biggest mistake anyone can make is the assumption that the China market is the same as any other, only bigger.

The market may be the same in some ways. After all, they want to buy low and sell high like everyone else. That is where the similarity ends, however. The social things we feel cost time and money are things they feel are worth the investment. The emphasis we put on our words and on verbal shorthand is, to the Chinese, vulgar and undignified. Doing business in China—for the Chinese—is a lifestyle, a ritual; it can't be rushed. It shouldn't be rushed, because it is what we *do*.

For many of us in the West, a job is a job, something we have to do to make a living. That is largely the result of the industrial revolution, which made humans mere cogs in a vast machinery of production. China is still pretty far behind where the industrial revolution is concerned. Oh, they have factories—some of them still running ancient Soviet-era equipment—and they have people working like automatons on assembly lines just like the rest of the world, but there is a difference in approach. They are realistic about what they do, and what their role is in the larger scheme of things.

For instance, it was not unusual in the days of the "iron rice bowl" when everyone had a guaranteed job for life to see workers lounging around, doing nothing. The cliché of the Chinese office worker, as an example, is that of a man or woman sitting at a desk, drinking tea from a jelly jar, and reading the newspaper. Slowly.

The only time you saw workers work on an assembly or production line was when there was a delegation visiting the place for an inspection tour. Then, the factory was a hive of activity. Once I had the experience of passing through one of those factories, watching the laborers and production personnel put their equipment through its paces, when I realized I had forgotten my notebook. I had left it on top of a stack of boxes. I went back into the factory to retrieve it and saw the workers—who, only seconds before, had been industrious and focused—sitting around, smoking cigarettes, and chatting.

The show of labor was just that, a show.

In those bad old days, waiters and waitresses in China could hardly be counted upon to serve you, since tipping was against the law. Thus, you would enter a restaurant and watch as a dozen waitpersons stood against the wall and studiously ignored you. It would take fifteen or twenty minutes before you would get a menu, and another twenty—no exaggeration—to get someone to take your order, which they did with a sigh and an annoyed expression as you cut into their daydream. (This would not happen if there were Party officials around, of course. One day, I was having dinner with my interpreter who happened to be a Party member. We waited and waited, and then she simply leaned back and with a bored air said the one word that was guaranteed to get an immediate response: *tongzhi*, "comrade"! The waiters jumped away from the wall and hovered around us, getting us menus, tea, napkins, whatever we wanted. Only a Party member would have had the nerve to utter the word "comrade" that way, so it behooved the waiters to pay attention since their futures were at stake. A bad word from the Party, and they would be waiting tables in a prison cafeteria in Tibet for the rest of their lives. It was an education.)

In another case, Anthony and I went to visit some factories in his home province, Shandong. We were quoting pharmaceutical equipment to one factory and silicon carbide rod manufacturing equipment to another. As it turned out, both factories were "New Life" institutes: i.e., prisons.

In China, prisons are factories. Prisoners are expected to pay for themselves by making their prisons turn a profit, manufacturing various goods and engaging in productive work. We may say that it is a form of slave labor, but in the United States we currently have two million people in prison—the highest percentage in the world—who were sent there to be "rehabilitated" and yet they are not learning any new trades or shown how "legal" capitalism really works. (Making license plates doesn't count.)

Thus, we were taken on a tour of a maximum security facility, complete with guard towers, searchlights, and men with automatic weapons. The prisoners themselves had actually been removed. We did not see a single one. We were led through various rooms—including a music room, with dust on the instruments and violins lacking strings—and finally as we were being led away, our guide, a young male interpreter who was eager to impress his overseas guests (quite a novelty at a maximum security prison in China) made the unintentionally funny and unintentionally chilling pronouncement: "Isn't this place wonderful? It's almost like Paradise. Why, it almost makes you want to commit a crime, just to get sent here!"

We made the mistake of repeating this man's words at the banquet we had with the Governor of Shandong Province, mentioned previously. We thought it was funny. The Governor was not amused, but he said nothing more about it that night.

The following morning, on our way back to Beijing, a representative of the Governor met us at the train station.

"The Governor sends his best wishes for a speedy and safe ride back to Beijing," he told us, with all the formal unctuousness of a sophisticated bureaucrat. "And he wishes you to know that the interpreter you mentioned has been reassigned, to a post in Xinjiang Province." And with that, he bowed and left us standing and staring open-mouthed after him.

The governor had been embarrassed by the careless remark of his interpreter, and by our careless remarks concerning him we had doomed the hapless cadre to a life in the most remote and forbidding landscape China has to offer. From that moment on, we kept our reactions to ourselves and never again said a word against anyone until we were safely alone and free from listening devices.

Alertness means not only paying attention to anything directly related to your project or your sales campaign; it means paying close attention to your surroundings and never forgetting where you are. China is a totalitarian regime. Communism may mean the "dictatorship of the proletariat" but I don't see many Chinese banging their shoes on the table, or giving orders to the Central Committee. The Communist Party has tremendous power in the country, and although the situation is a lot looser today than it was in the 1980s and 1990s, it can just as easily swing back to the days of paranoia and repression. The arrest of Chen Liangyu may have been a signal to the other wheeler-dealers that the Party was still in control and still called all the shots.

Do not be distracted by the amusements China has to offer the foreign businessman with hard currency in his wallet. In the first place, China *owns* your hard currency. At this time—in the year 2007—China has more than one trillion dollars of foreign exchange reserves in its banks, the world's largest such reserves. That means that they have been loaning money to other countries, including yours. Chinese investment in banks, real estate, and stocks in the United States has reached such a level that if the US were to go bankrupt, China would be ruined. At this moment, the value of the Chinese *yuan*—also known as RMB or *Ren Min Bi*, their equivalent of the US dollar—is pegged at about eight to the US dollar, where it has been for years. Everyone knows that the value of the *yuan* is closer to four to the US dollar, but revaluing the *yuan* would cause serious dislocation in the money markets of the world. While it would double the value of money kept in Chinese banks and make the average Chinese worker "doubly happy," it would also reduce China's ability to compete in the world market by making its exports twice as expensive. Hence, the reluctance of the Chinese government—which controls China's banks—to revalue the *yuan*. If they do, when they do, it will be gradual and take place over years. So, your currency these days is not as attractive as it once was.

In the second place, the presence of China's dread Public Security Bureau is ubiquitous, and it is an arm of the Party. You do not want to be a foreigner caught breaking the law in China. They do not follow the maxim of

suck *now,* and their equipment and machinery be laugh-able *now,* and the man you thought was the factory's jani-tor is actually its general manager . . . but the China of today is vastly different from the China of only twenty years ago. They've come a long way, baby, and they are moving fast. Do not underestimate the people sitting politely in front of you in the freezing, unheated confer-ence room with their chapped red hands wrapped around what appear to be children's notebooks. These individuals are in charge of multimillion-dollar enterprises today, and will be the CEOs of China's new industries tomorrow. They are your *guanxi.* Cherish them. Treat them with dig-nity and honor and respect.

No matter how much they piss you off.

Attack when the opportunity presents itself. You will spend a lot of time in seemingly endless negotiations, but there will come a moment when you both know that the time has come to commit. Sometimes this moment takes place when word has reached you that your competitor has just made a misstep. Sometimes it happens when the local political boss shows up to find out what's taking so long. Sometimes it happens the day after you've left town, and your competitor has taken the contract.

My first year in China I stayed in Beijing during the Christmas holidays. Alone. I was a lonely figure in the Beijing Hotel, rolling around the cavernous lobby and drinking bad instant coffee in the coffee shop downstairs. But there was a method to my madness.

I had been competing with the Japanese on several projects. One of these was for high-voltage power cable for the city of Xi'an. The cable I was offering was made by Ericsson in Sweden, and the Swedish engineer (a man I will never forget, Olle Matteson) and I spent a grueling and very tiring two weeks at the technical negotiation where we had to show our cable was supe-rior to both the Italians and the Japanese. Our inter-preter at the time was a sweet young woman, fresh out of college, who could barely manage "hello," much less the complicated technical jargon of the electrical industry. One of the men present during the entire negotiation had a perfect command of English and of the jargon, but he refused to take part in the interpretation because it wasn't his job. Therefore, we all had to suffer.

Well, the technical part of the negotiation was accomplished and the engineer went home to Sweden. The commercial side, however, had not been done. It was December.

The customer—one of the utilities ministries—was taking his time. One week became another. I phoned home and told my family I was not going to make it back for Christmas. (They had a great time without me anyway, I am chagrined to admit!) I waited.

The Italians went home for the holidays.

The Japanese went home.

I was the only one left standing, in a bitterly cold northern Chinese winter, snowflakes swirling around my shoes, as I waited patiently for the day to arrive. Children in the West await Christmas morning with eagerness and keen expectation. China in the 1980s knew nothing of Christmas and didn't celebrate it as a holiday, certainly, and were unconcerned about its religious associations, as befitting a Communist regime.

Thus, I signed the power cable contract on Christmas Day 1986.

The Chinese had either just wanted to see who would wait around the longest, or they really had no idea that Christmas was special to the foreigners and had planned all along to sign it on Christmas Day with no idea of the irony: for me, my present that Christmas was a 1.6 million dollar contract for power cable, the first ever for Ericsson Power Cables in China and for the ancient capitol, Xi'an, at that.

If you are a person accustomed to luxury, comfort, and all the perks of international trade you would come to expect in the West, then China is not for you. It is not a comfortable place for a foreigner to do business. The infrastructure still needs work, although China is working like mad right now to improve all of that before the 2008 Olympics . . . but that's just in the main cities. If you go to the villages, you will find poor communications, poor transportation, questionable lodgings, and a lot of time spent waiting. There will be miscommunications, misunderstandings, and missed signals. You will be frustrated. You will be angry. You will be ready to pack it in and go home.

Don't. You are a guerrilla warrior, and this is your lot. Victory will be yours if you can conquer yourself first, and then China. Don't let your frustration show. Hide your anger. Smile. Wait patiently. Pay attention.

As Mao says, "Adjust to the enemy situation."

Chapter 5
The Fifth Stratagem

How are guerrilla bands formed?
—Chairman Mao

So far, we've discussed some of the issues in the China business environment, including culture, business rituals, the Communist influence in the market, and even the advantages and disadvantages of using an interpreter. What we have to address now are the practical matters of forming a team to execute your market strategy and win projects in this most difficult of "enemy terrains."

Your team will be composed of two main components: the support team in your home country, and the attack or "away" team in China. Both must function to maximum operating capacity, or you will find yourself going two steps forward and one step back on the long march, and this will only serve to increase your frustration with the market and amplify the lack of patience with your campaign among your colleagues back home.

The Home Team

Without the unswerving support of your home office, you will accomplish nothing in the long run. You may sign contracts, but you will not be able to fulfill them professionally and your reputation will be ruined. Thus, you must first concentrate on the people who stay behind and who have always worked to build your company. They will need to learn some new skills and develop a more flexible attitude toward things like paper flow and office hours. You will need to remember to reward them from time to time, to show your appreciation for their efforts above and beyond what they had been expected to do heretofore. They will either resist at first and then slowly come around to your way of thinking, or they will embrace the challenge at first and then become slowly discouraged and disenchanted with the whole process. It is rare that any company's employees will gladly take on a challenge such as China trade support and maintain that level of enthusiasm through the difficulties that will inevitably ensue. Those who resist at first are probably wiser, and the amount of work that you will do to win them over will be educational for you as well as for them because it will remind you of the strengths and weaknesses of your own organization: characteristics that support staff are often better equipped to judge than upper-level management. You must pay attention to them at this stage, because whether they are enthusiastic about the new opportunity or not, their reluctance at any point will highlight those areas that you need to address before you can confidently build your "away team."

The areas you need to look at first are obvious: **marketing and advertising**, because you will need media that is appropriate for the China market (i.e., you cannot simply "port" your existing brochures, etc. as-is for China). **Manufacturing**, because you will need to change some of the specifications of your existing product offering for China: some of this is due to different electrical systems (50 Hz versus 60 Hz, for instance), but also the Chinese will want other changes or modifications to suit different environmental requirements peculiar to their working situation. In some cases, excesses of heat, moisture, dust, etc. are common in many Chinese worksites; these factors can wreak havoc with sensitive equipment, and often engineers who are used to the Western working environment do not suspect that their machinery will face tougher challenges anywhere else. The Chinese will often demand greater resilience from your products, especially in the areas of extremes of temperature and humidity, as well as dust.

The **shipping** department will be subject to a different level of stress, as well. The documentation required for international shipments are already onerous; when you factor in China and the details of letters of credit and other contract documentation, it becomes bewildering. Your shipping personnel must be conversant with international shipping procedures and requirements. There are several schools and institutes that specialize in training courses for companies getting involved in international shipping, and it would be a good idea to send your people to take such a course before you get too involved in China (or any foreign market, for that matter). Documentation is not the only thing to be reconsidered, however; packaging is another issue that has to be investigated. One thing you do not want to experience is having your delicate equipment shipped to China only to arrive damaged in some way due to poor or inadequate packaging. Your packers and shippers have to understand that delivery to China can take place through a series of air, ground, and ocean segments and that the packaging has to be able to stand up to all of that. The cost of replacing damaged equipment—or of going to China yourself to inspect the shipment—can be prohibitive, especially if there are timelines built into your contract.

The **accounting** department will be feeling the pain, too. New methods of payment will tax their patience; the peculiarities of the letter of credit, the letter of assignment of proceeds, and other documentation that has to be prepared precisely, with no typographical errors, requires a methodical, tranquil approach and excellent record-keeping skills. Letters of credit expire; it has been my experience that a letter of credit for several hundred thousand dollars lay uncollected in the bottom of a bookkeeper's drawer at one of my companies until it was way past its expiration date. When that happens, there is little you can do except go back to the issuer—your customer—and basically beg him to open another L/C or somehow extend the old one so that you can collect payment. There are classes on the L/C given at various financial institutions, and this would be a good investment, as well.

Some companies also invest in **export insurance**. Basically, this is a policy that protects your company in the event your overseas customers do not pay their invoices. In the case of China trade, I have not found this to be useful if only because all of my business in China was handled by L/Cs; however, your accounting and legal experts may prevail upon you to get this insurance anyway. Usually, it is calculated as a percentage of your export business.

Your **engineering** department will be called upon to make changes in some of your products. You will work with them first, and then the changes will pass to manufacturing. It is important that you maintain a good relationship with your company's engineers, for you will be contacting them constantly from China to ask how a certain modification will affect the product or if it is even possible. They need to be on-board with your China campaign and to realize its importance to your company.

If you provide training in the use or application of your products, then you need to collaborate with the **training** department as well. Training materials will have to be provided in Chinese, and possibly trainers sent to China to give hands-on instruction. Your trainers (and other personnel you will be sending overseas) will have to be instructed as to how to conduct themselves in China. You will very probably be their instructor, so you will have to have a basic lesson plan prepared that will cover cultural, linguistic, and business issues. It is important that all the work you have done so far to create goodwill in China will not be undone by careless actions or remarks by staff you have brought over to help in your campaign.

Unfortunately, I can personally attest to several examples of how American engineers and trainers—once in China—created havoc with my staff and customers. In spite of the steps I had taken to ensure that there would be no problems, I was faced with some of the difficulties you can expect when bringing people to China for the first time, and in this case people who are not burdened with achieving a sales target but who are there in a support capacity and thus feel freer to indulge their fantasies at your expense!

Don't pour cold water on the scientists. We want active elements to remain active. Even when sometimes their work isn't done well, we shouldn't pour cold water, but should help them correct their mistakes. Only those individual, extremely stubborn and incurable, elements should be handled differently ...

—Chairman Mao

In the first case, I had an engineer who worked for the training department who was rather young and inexperienced in overseas travel. Although married, he formed a close personal attachment to one of the women on my staff in Beijing (who was also married) when he was brought over to conduct training for our staff and customers. His romantic liaison led to his divulging information to the young woman concerning pay levels back in the States. When she learned that she was being paid far less in China than she would had she lived in the States, she became angry and began pressuring the trainer to marry her and take her back with him to America.

One of the reasons we were able to have a staff in China was due to lower salary expectations. The cost of living in China, for a local national, is far less than what it is for a foreigner (whose living quarters were segregated from the rest of the population due to security considerations and who thus lived in costly apartments and, due to their lack of Mandarin, wound up eating in expensive establishments that catered to foreigners). If I had to pay American wages in China, I would not have been able to hire anyone at all. The Chinese may understand this, intellectually, but no one likes having this rubbed in their face. This was made worse by the sheer stupidity of the trainer who expressed his own outrage to the woman that she was being paid less than her opposite number in the States.

The engineer wound up disappearing every day after office hours. This is a dangerous situation in China, and as it turned out his actions were nothing short of suicidal. He not only abandoned his duties as an engineer—who typically must attend the same evening banquets with customers as the rest of us—but when we did not know where he was or whom he was with, it increased our anxiety levels. A foreigner can get into a lot of trouble in China, especially one who is enamored of one of the local women. Sexual liaisons may be as common in China as they are anywhere else, but when a foreigner is involved there are all sorts of other issues, including a suspicion of prostitution. Foreign engineers have been arrested by the Public Security Bureau and deported when they are caught *in flagrante* with a local woman. This is not a common occurrence, but it does happen. Although the situation has improved considerably now, ten years ago when the engineer decided to vanish for a weekend as he followed his lady to her hometown he was in danger of being not only arrested, but even murdered by the lady's husband! A foreigner stands out in small-town China: one can go nowhere without literally hundreds of people being aware of one's movements. There is no privacy for a foreigner there, so your actions are subject to all sorts of observation and—at times—reports to the PSB.

We had to send the engineer home, and I was forced to fire the woman who simply refused to work but insisted on showing up every day anyway. It was not a pleasant task, for I had known her for several years and valued her contribution, but she became bitter and angry

. . . and a total disruption to our office's already delicate emotional status.

Another trainer did the same thing while I was away in another city. He would ask the staff members personal questions about their salaries, and then mock them for making so little! He tried to turn the workers against their general manager, and he tried to turn my home office against me by stating that I was not "American enough." When I complained to his boss back in the States after I sent him packing, I was told that his boss—who had never been to China—knew more about China than did I who had spent half a lifetime there.

I mention these two incidents so that you understand what you may face within your own ranks once the China card is on the table. Some of your male personnel may harbor all sorts of fantasies concerning Asian women, and this can lead to trouble for them and for you. While there are many websites and books that discuss expats abroad and their relationships with women in Thailand, the Philippines, and China (among other locales) and the problems that come with these relationships, none address the question of what happens if the expat is working for an American company at the time: a company that is depending on the expat's focus and professionalism.

Also, once members of your home office have gone abroad for the first time, they can find the experience exhilarating and addictive. They will conspire and agitate for another trip, politicking the office like a Washington lobbyist. This has nothing to do with the success of your company or supporting the company's goals; it has everything to do with personal agendas and particularly with the opportunity to be out of the office and far away from home.

I have nothing against personal agendas. We all have them. But you cannot allow them to disrupt your company's very expensive penetration of the China market. All the time and effort you put into building a reputation there can be torpedoed in an instant by a dazzled staff member. Our office in Beijing was rocked by these events, and had a hard time recovering from them, despite the fact that our staff was paid higher salaries than their counterparts working for our competitors and also had incentives built into their compensation. The bad feelings and resentment that these two self-absorbed individuals caused us meant that we had to work that much harder to get the operation back on track.

There is one more element to your home team that you have to consider.

You need a **permanent liaison** between your home team and your away team. There has to be someone based in your home office who will coordinate the activities of all the other departments relative to China, and who will serve as your contact point. It is extremely difficult to handle the amount of email, fax, and phone traffic to each individual department on your own from China. If you have one contact person inside who will receive all the communications and manage your China business efficiently and competently then you have created a kind of clone of yourself who knows what is going on in China and can ensure that the domestic side of your operation runs smoothly. This is very important, and you should identify this person as early as possible, as you will rely upon him or her in the months to follow.

Once the various departments at home have been organized and briefed on what is to come, you have to concentrate on the team you have set up in China. This is where you have to get a little creative and maintain that degree of alertness and mobility we talked about in the last chapter.

The Away Team

This is your guerrilla band. These are the individuals who will work hard and achieve incredible things. This team does not have to be large in number, but it has to be expert in what it does and it has to be keenly motivated.

Like a guerrilla band, this team has to consist of several competencies. One of these is the intelligence function. This individual is probably the one who got you into China trade in the first place. It may be a sales agent or a sales representative. It may be an entrepreneur who is based in China and who is looking for foreign business partners in a joint venture or other commercial relationship. You may have been contacted by this person by mail, or email or fax, looking for information about your company for a possible project in China. Or you may have been referred to this person by a colleague or someone at your local chamber of commerce or by your Commerce Department's own trade office, which maintains extensive trade contacts in more than a hundred foreign countries around the world.

Possibly you were more pro-active, and placed an ad—in Chinese—in an overseas trade journal, actively seeking partners or sales agents.

However this happened, you have built a tentative relationship with an individual who claims to know where there are projects ripe for the taking. Here is a word of advice, then:

A professional sales agent or sales representative will not ask for money up front. They will always consider a percentage of the profit, a piece of the action. Ordinarily, this will be ten percent, but it could be more or less depending on the size of the project and the difficulty of winning it for your company. You will establish the parameters of this relationship up front, in writing. Your agent will then be guaranteed his or her share of the net or the gross in the project(s) undertaken on your behalf. In this case, agents are motivated to see the project through to a successful completion, as they won't get paid until after the contract is signed and fulfilled.

If you are approached by someone asking for front money, walk away. That agent can ask a dozen companies for front money and then win the contract for a competitor. There is no loyalty in this business that is not blessed by a legal document and the binding promise of future remuneration. Be smart and do not fall for the glittering assurances of a confidence man who can dazzle you with his stories of past glory and seem like a man of the world . . . when he is really a man of the underworld.

However, if you have identified a reliable individual who is willing to work for you and ensure that you win the project he has in mind, then you are indeed fortunate and you should throw your resources behind him. In the future, this person may very well become the lead operative in your China-based team. He may never work as an official employee of your company—for all sorts of legal and economic reasons—but he will nonetheless work for you once you have established yourself as reliable and your company as a manufacturer of world-class product. It will be in his best interests to maintain a good relationship with you and your company because your market penetration is also *his* market penetration. He gains prestige and power in the market with every successful job he wins for you.

Will he make money on the side, though?

Some companies object to having an agent work for them who is doing other business, or who has other "arrangements" that are not covered by their contract. They feel this is a conflict of interest, or somehow ethically (if not legally) wrong. My reaction has always been "so what?" If the agent or representative is doing a good job for your company, it doesn't matter if he or she has side arrangements with your customers or has other business that does not impact on yours. This only becomes a concern when the side business or side arrangements impact negatively on your strategy, in which case there needs to be a discussion about how to proceed. Normally, your agent will not openly discuss any such arrangements: this is something you find out through rumor or gossip, or from a "disgruntled former employee" with an axe to grind. Personally, this has never bothered me for the simple reason that a happy agent is a good agent; if he or she is getting additional compensation while working for you, then the chances are that the agent will be loyal to your firm for purely mercenary reasons: there is no need to kill the goose that lays the golden eggs, neither for the agent nor for you. I do caution, however, that a situation like this bears watching. Once the agent seems to lose interest in your business, is difficult to locate during the day, doesn't answer the phone or return calls, or otherwise behaves in a suspicious manner, then you may have a problem on your hands. Either he or she is planning on a move to another firm—or even another industry—or there is some dissatisfaction with the existing arrangement. If the agent understands that you have no problem with outside business as long as your own strategy proceeds in an orderly fashion, then there should be no need for acrimony.

You need to support this person as much as possible. You cannot expect an agent to function at full capacity if there is a lack of technical or commercial resources. That means you must first listen to the agent describe the requirements of the market, and then work out a plan for providing logistical support. And this support *must* be forthcoming, and it must be provided according to the pre-arranged timetable. Any slacking off on your side will result in the agent not trusting your commitment to the market, or your ability to produce what is needed. Your agent is also a kind of customer, a consumer of your services and support, and you should treat him or her that way and with the same degree of seriousness and respect. You should not expect the agent to work miracles on her own; her utility rests in the ability to identify potential customers and to navigate the Chinese business environment, saving you time and money and resources in the process. This cannot be accomplished without the same level of support you would give to any of your salespersons in your home country; in fact, the level of support required in China is considerably greater, although not considerably more costly.

For instance, printed materials must be provided, as much as possible, and in a format useful for the market. If the agent insists that the brochures or other technical or sales-oriented information be printed in Chinese—and this is virtually a certainty—then you must work with the agent to ensure that the best quality translation is made. In the past, I have never used a domestic translation service for this function; instead, I have relied upon the agent to source a translator or translation service in China. This is for two reasons: in the first place, I am reassured that the translation is one that is appropriate to the Chinese market (as opposed to the overseas Chinese market); in the second place, it is a lot cheaper to source this kind of service in China than in the West. Further, I will normally provide artwork for the brochures to the agent so that the Chinese version can be printed in China, which is also much cheaper than having it printed in the States or Europe, plus you save the cost and time of shipping heavy printed material overseas and getting it through customs. The quality of print media in China is very high; many American publishers use Chinese print houses and art designers already, and this practice will only grow in the future.

Now, it is entirely possible that the agent will add an additional ten percent or more to the cost of translation and printing for him- or herself; you will never know this and, once again, who cares? If the agent makes money on doing this service for your company, and the cost is still much lower than it would be for you to get the same job done in your country, *who cares*? You would be surprised to know how many companies *do* care, however, and regard the agent with renewed suspicion. This is a waste of time and deflects your attention away from the real goal. Your purpose in China is not to be some kind of moral guardian or ethics police; your goal is to get your products sold and to be profitable and successful in this exhilarating market. And, let's face it, your agent is Chinese and has relatives in China who are involved in all sorts of businesses. If some of the printing and translation work (for example) gets passed to a relative (*guanxi*!), you will never know anyway, so sit back and relax.

Marketing support will also take the form of a list of your existing or past customers. Some of these may be companies that your Chinese clients will recognize, and this is very useful because if they have not heard of you or your company they will certainly recognize some of your other clients and this will increase their comfort level. Scour your records for the orders you have booked with name-brand companies, whether in your home country or in other countries around the world. This list should be provided to your agent as soon as possible in the relationship.

Details concerning the education level and previous employment of some of your key employees may also be useful. If your CEO is a graduate of Harvard or Yale, this will be impressive; if one of your engineers worked for a Fortune 500 company or got his PhD at MIT, this also looks good on your corporate profile. The number of patents your company owns, the white papers you've published, the technological advances you've made . . . all of this is important. Copies of some of these would be useful to impress potential clients in China.

A portfolio of ads you have run in the trade journals will also help the Chinese gauge the relative strength of your company vis-à-vis the industry in general. And a well-crafted website is also very important: it will be the first time many of your clients will "meet" your company, and it should look as professional as possible and be easy to navigate around. And, if you are able to provide a web page in Chinese, so much the better. (Although this is not necessary right now, with the explosive growth of the Chinese end of the Internet, a Chinese-language web page will enable Chinese search engines to find your company before they find your competitors; thus, my advice is to consider this tactic seriously because it could give you an edge early on. As requests for more information come in—in Chinese—they can be handed over to your agent in China for action, thus relieving you of the responsibility of hiring a Chinese-language expert in-house.)

Price lists. This is a sensitive part of your strategy, and it must be thought out carefully in advance and the basic tactic adhered to by everyone involved. Pricing for China is a moveable feast; your competitors in China have established a price platform already. In many cases, they will be charging more in China than they do elsewhere, especially if the market is relatively new for your products. In other cases, though, and especially if the market is mature, the pricing levels for China will be lower than your own country. You need to be able to find a way to accommodate those lower prices and still maintain profitability. We will examine all of this in more detail in the chapters that follow, but for now keep this in mind:

If you publish a price list, it is never considered a final offer. A price list in China is a basis for negotiation. They will compare your price list against others they already have. Thus, it is important for you to acquire those lists and this is one of the jobs you give your agent. You need to look at these lists and ensure that your published price list does not deviate too much from theirs. You don't want to appear grossly higher or grossly lower; you want to be in their ballpark. If your prices seem too high at first, there will be a tendency to ignore them in favor of the "(foreign) devil they know." If your prices seem too low, there will be a tendency to believe that your products are not made in your home country, but in some developing nation's factory in, say, Bangladesh, Mexico, or . . . China. The premium attraction of your product is its foreign origin. There is an assumption that goods produced in Western countries are somehow superior in quality than goods made locally. This is changing, of course, as more and more Chinese factories begin producing goods of world-class quality, using the latest in quality control equipment and methods, but total adoption of international quality standards is still a long way off for many companies. So, my advice is not to price your products too low. Remember, the negotiations are yet to come and deep discounts will be demanded anyway.

If you don't publish a price list—if you are an engineering company, for instance, or some kind of consulting firm, architectural firm, or software engineering firm (as examples)—then the clients will still want to know where you stand in terms of cost to them. Some examples from your past work will help. However, much of that information is proprietary, so it would be best to work up a kind of sample proposal that can be used to position your company not only in terms of its pricing structure but also in terms of its capability. Thus, technical and commercial information in one package can be used to impress your clients and give them enough data to appreciate your firm's professionalism. Of course, the Chinese will also use that package to get similar "quotes" from your competitors. The temptation will be too great not to do so! Therefore, you should be careful to make the package general enough so that specifics of your technology and methodology are not revealed to your competitors. This is a "teaser" package, and as such should not give the whole show away.

You must also consider samples. If you sell components or parts, this is easy. You send your agent a representative collection of your product line; as many individual pieces as possible, and not only one of each but several. The Chinese need to see the product, hold it, and examine it. Which brings us to the next point: these samples must be *perfect*. You cannot send subquality or nonfunctioning parts to China; this is not only a waste of time, but it will negatively impact your company's reputation. Whatever you send to China must be in perfect operating condition and it must be flawless in appearance. There is a tendency to "dump" second-rate parts as samples, not only in China but pretty much everywhere on the assumption that everyone knows it's "just a sample" and that the final product supplied will be much better. There is no such assumption in China; if your customers see a substandard part, they will associate you and your company with that substandard part. So . . . make sure the samples you supply are first quality, and that you have shipped them carefully to avoid freight damage. You would be surprised how often samples arrive in China in damaged condition due to poor packaging at the factory, which means that all the time and money spent in getting them there is totally wasted. Timing is everything, as Mao and every other guerrilla leader was aware. If your samples arrive late, you can lose a contract. If you arrive late, you can lose a contract. If your pricing arrives late . . . well, you get the picture. The picture, but not the contract.

Personnel. This is another issue and it can be costly, in more ways than one. There will come a time—sooner rather than later—when it is necessary to wave the flag. Your clients will want to see the people in your company whom they will rely upon for production and support. They want to see mature, reasonable, professional individuals at the top of their field. If you are the China guru in your company, the clients will have already met you and are comfortable with you, but they now want to see the other people behind you: the engineers and the top level executives (in the case that you are not the CEO or the Managing Director or General Manager yourself). This is for two reasons: in the first place, they want to be reassured that you have the in-house competence to handle their orders; in the second place, they want to know that your company values them highly enough to send your very best, your chief executives as well as your top engineers. This means that the relationship will be strong because it is valued so highly.

When it comes to large-scale projects involving installations of equipment or computer networks, cabling, etc. then it will always be necessary to send someone of the requisite competence to the site in China to oversee the work. Before the contract is signed, the Chinese may insist on such a clause so that they know the installation will be a shared responsibility between their company and yours. The cost of sending that person or persons must therefore be factored into the total cost of the project.

But "personnel" does not only cover *your* personnel. This is China, and an essential element of many Chinese contracts with foreign firms is the visit by the Chinese delegation to your country.

The Chinese—like everyone else—love to travel abroad. For many years it was almost impossible to do so, due to the internal political situation. It has become much easier now, in the years since the death of Deng Xiao Ping, but it is still expensive for the Chinese. Therefore, quite often it has become a part of the contract to include the costs for a group of personnel from the Chinese side to visit your country. You can negotiate the number of people you will host, and for how long, and where . . . but usually the junket involves some sight-seeing and some shopping, as well as a perfunctory visit to your factory for an "inspection."

When they do arrive, they must be treated as honored guests. You must provide transportation, meals, etc. They will have no clue as to how to go about doing any of this on their own; this will usually be the first visit to your country for many of them, and they will be unused to the system and the culture. They will also have a hard time eating Western food: generally speaking, Chinese do not like cheese or other dairy products. Some have a hard time with steak, as anyone who has spent a few months in China eating with chopsticks can understand. Of course, the urban, sophisticated Chinese are way past all that but there is a better than even chance that your customers will be from the countryside and be unused to Western cuisine and culture. You have to be sensitive to these differences and make sure that you have a Chinese restaurant in your area lined up with advance warning that you will be bringing people over from China and to prepare regular Chinese—not "Chinese-American"— food for their arrival.

When you have come this far with your customer, they have become in effect part of your "guerrilla band": you have formed an alliance with them, and you should treat them as comrades and friends, engaged in a common struggle for victory. For you, the victory is measured in terms of profitability and market share; oddly enough, for them it may be the same. They may be using your technology and your products to improve their presence in their own market or even, in some cases, to penetrate foreign markets as well. You should be pro-active in this regard. If there is a way to help them in their own business strategy you should be available to do so; it is better to have them on your side now than to fight against them later on. You may find yourself in a joint venture with them some day, collaborating in a new market that you would never have been able to penetrate on your own.

Chapter 6
The Sixth Stratagem

What is meant by initiative in warfare? In all battles and wars, a struggle to gain and retain the initiative goes on between the opposing sides, for it is the side that holds the initiative that has the liberty of action.

—Chairman Mao

With the formation of the "guerrilla band"—the elements of your domestic operation working in tandem with your China-based team—you now have to approach the market from a revolutionary perspective.

The goal of Chairman Mao was, obviously, to defeat both the Japanese invaders and the government of Generalissimo Chiang Kai-Shek of the Kuomintang. In other words, his immediate goal was the same as that of every revolutionary and every politician: absolute political power for his party and himself. His long-term goal was to create a perfect socialist state and a paragon of Communism.

Your immediate goal in China is not very different from that of Chairman Mao: you want absolute control of the market for yourself and your company. Your tactics must reflect those of Chairman Mao in order to be successful:

the "alertness, mobility and attack" we discussed earlier. Your long-term goal is the strengthening of your company as a whole; if your China strategy detracts from your company's overall strength and position, then it is not working. Of course, in the short term, your China project will deplete resources and strain some of your company's internal structure, but that should only be a temporary problem as your company gets its "sea legs" and accommodates itself to the new reality of doing business abroad in general and in China specifically. If your China project continues to apply stress to the corporate structure and detract from the bottom line after two years, then it is time to reassess your position.

That being said, let us now look at some specifics as to how you will be able to employ your guerrilla band in the field. Remember that the initiative is yours: you have the "liberty of action" as Mao wrote, but not for long. Your competitors will eventually see that you are in the market and pose a potential threat. They will attempt to regain the initiative through all sorts of maneuvers that they would consider unethical in the West but which, in China, they somehow deem justified.

The Agent

> **Who are our enemies? Who are our friends? This is a question of the first importance for the revolution.**
>
> **—Chairman Mao**

Your first attempt at getting a sale in China will be largely educational. If you are lucky, the agent who contacted you will already have a few projects and customers in mind otherwise he wouldn't have contacted you in the first place. In these tender few moments of the honeymoon between agent and company, it is possible—indeed, likely—that the agent has already contacted a few of your competitors, too. He is keeping all of you working, to see which one will be the most competitive, have the best product line, and be the most willing to come to terms and support the market. It is up to you to realize that this is happening and to compete for your agent's attention. He or she is actually your first client in China: if you win the sale to the agent, you are in a good position to win the sale to the actual customer. It's the beginning of a beautiful friendship.

If you have not been contacted by someone in China yet, then it is up to you to stir the pot a little. As mentioned previously, there are various ways of doing this short of actually traveling to China and looking around. (I have done some cold-calling in places like Hong Kong and Singapore . . . where such an approach is considered distinctly odd, especially coming from a foreigner. In Beijing or Shanghai, however, it would be almost impossible to do because business in China is a formal affair and no one simply "drops in." One could leave brochures here and there in the offices of potential clients, but that is probably a waste of time.)

You can identify some sales representatives and sales agents through your local Commerce Department office. Your government probably has a commercial attaché in China who can help you identify some likely candidates. There are also a number of Chinese companies that act as sourcing agents for a variety of local firms; your government office can help you with these, too.

However, the government can only be helpful so far. Their information is often a little out-dated or simply not appropriate for your needs, depending on how active your government is in helping promote trade with China and if they are willing to help a small business such as yours. In any case, though, approaching the local commercial attaché will get you in the door and get the pump primed.

Another possibility consists of reading the trade journals. Some of your competitors already have business in China and this will be mentioned in the trades. You will glean some useful information from these articles, such as the location of the projects they won, the names of local contact people, the name of the Chinese government office or agency involved, etc. If you are clever, you can use that information to pry out other details or you can even approach the article-writer to get some deeper background information.

Another approach is more subtle, but it works.

If you are a manufacturer of, say, computer cable and you are looking for potential customers in China, you can approach a Chinese manufacturer of copper wire—a component of computer cable—with the idea that you will source copper wire from them if they can help you identify potential customers. I am not suggesting you deceive the Chinese manufacturer; rather, sourcing copper wire locally and making the cable in China will give you a distinct edge over imported brands in terms of cost, so the relationship could easily be viable. If you never get to that point, however, the discussions with the Chinese manufacturer will give you some important market intelligence. Therefore, seek out local manufacturers that would be the counterparts to your suppliers in your home country; they often have a very good grasp of market conditions, upcoming projects, and the nature of your competition. Be careful not to reveal too much about your plans and strategies to them, however! They can be relied upon to trade some of that information back to your competitors, especially if they feel it will help them increase their profile and get them some additional business. There may also be someone at that company who has relatives or friends inside a competitor's operation (*guanxi*!) and will inform them, secretly, of the new development.

Mao's guerrillas also knew the value of what his Soviet comrades called *disinformatsiya,* or "disinformation." You can sometimes use this ploy to find out if there is a mole in your company, your agent's, or one of your customers. It consists of giving out some false information to a select individual or individuals just to see where it will wind up. Like the dye that is used to trace a chemical's path in the human body, disinformation's path will show you who is leaking, and to whom. This cannot be used too often, however, for people will get wise to the tactic and cover their traces.

Assuming you now have someone in China helping you find your first contract, how should this relationship be managed? First, the agent will ask you for a lot of information about your company and about its specific product offerings. There will be demands for brochures and technical data and samples. This is all reasonable. There will also be requests for your client list: satisfied customers and the general nature of their business relationship with you in terms of size of business, length of time they've been your customer, etc. This is also reasonable, exactly what you would expect from any sales rep in your own country.

There will also be an almost immediate request to know your price levels, and this is where you have to exercise caution as mentioned in the last chapter. You can give budgetary pricing, i.e., some suggestive, "ball park" pricing without revealing your profit margins or how low you are willing to go. You only need to get serious about pricing when you are down to the wire in a negotiation and have successfully passed the technical phase of the discussions.

With all of this background established, you are ready for your first foray into the market. The agent is now deployed and has identified one or two—or more—likely projects. You are ready to take the initiative in the field.

The First Foray

You need to hit the ground running in order to seize the initiative, but you need to keep running in order to maintain it. You need to appear as heavily supported as the larger companies you are up against, but in this first phase of your strategy you do not want to get their attention. Not yet. You don't have the strength to fight them hand-to-hand or face-to-face. Hence, the advice given earlier about using the villages to encircle the cities. The villages are not only geographical places on the Chinese map, they are also virtual locations: projects and customers that are remote from your competitor's market strategy. The way you enter this market will tell everyone a great deal about you and your capabilities . . . and your strategy. You need to create comfort in your customers, but confusion in your enemy, about these very concepts.

The Chinese market is unique in several ways. You can take advantage of these differences because they will certainly work in your favor if you are clever. One difference is in the way the market follows the leader.

You need to have several projects going at once. That is, you need to be quoting on the small projects but you also need to be quoting the larger, seemingly inaccessible jobs as well. Your major focus will be on the small jobs, while your competitor will be focusing on the big win: the large, high-profile job that is worth millions while your smaller jobs may be worth a few hundred thousand each, at most. The Chinese generally fear the risk of taking on a new supplier, particularly an overseas supplier. This goes to a lot of anti-Western propaganda promoted by Mao and others in the Chinese government over the past fifty years or so, but also is due to China's experience with foreigners and the way they have trampled China's dignity. This is a fact, and it cannot be avoided or white-washed. Further, there are definite dangers to working with you: if your customer chooses you over a better-known, more well-established company then they risk a charge of being either incompetent or being somehow corrupted into the relationship through bribery. If the project fails, you lose your reputation but the customer may very well lose his freedom or even his life. Therefore, the burden is on you to prove your worthiness.

The upside of this is that once you have won a small project you have made it easier to win a larger project. That is because the Chinese "follow the leader": if they know that another company has taken the chance on you, their liability in the eyes of the Party is thereby diminished. The next company can always point the finger at your first customer and claim that they had been led astray. This is the real domino theory in action.

Suddenly, after you have won one or two smaller jobs in China you are in a better position to win the larger project. This is because you will be viewed as a novelty, someone they can control a little better because your competitors have been calling the shots all this time and monopolized the territory. With you in the picture, your customers have more leverage and more freedom to choose. As you take the initiative, you defeat your competitor in the field he thought was his.

Sometimes, these projects overlap and you find yourself with an embarrassment of riches. Literally.

A case in point:

In 1996, I was the vice president in charge of international sales for the American manufacturer of structured cabling components. We had targeted a major, high-profile project in Beijing. It was worth millions, not just in terms of the contract itself but in the amount of other business it would bring us if we won it. Our major competitor was ATT, but we also had a number of other strong players in the market.

We were unknown in China at the time. We did not have a single project. We hardly even had an office: we were operating out of a hotel room near the Beijing Railway Station.

We were quoting on a number of projects, among them the new headquarters for China Telecom. We were in a very good position to win the smaller project as we had *guanxi* in the Beijing Phone Company. If you don't work with the Beijing Phone Company in Beijing, you don't get a dial tone. Wisely, we had focused on the decision-maker in the phone company as our first priority.

This man had a small office in a building that by Western standards would have been condemned. By now it probably has been. He held court at his desk, with a bench full of supplicants lining one wall in the narrow room. This included the president of a university who had had the temerity to install a new wing and wired it without prior approval of the phone company. The man at the desk—whose title was not great, but whose authority in this single matter of who gets service and when was absolute—told the university president that he could do nothing, because he had not been consulted on the project in the first place.

Then it was our turn.

It was September. The Autumn Festival, as it is officially known in China but the Mooncake Festival as it is known everywhere else in the Chinese diaspora. We had brought a stack of packages of moon cakes for the phone company official, gaily wrapped and tied up with ribbons. We spoke with the man for about ten minutes or so. That was all it took.

When we returned to the negotiation table, we had the prior approval of the phone company and would be assured of getting a dial tone once our installation was complete. Even further, we cut a deal so that the installers themselves would be employees of . . . the Beijing Phone Company. With that relationship cemented, we were able to give our customer something the other guys had not thought of: additional security and peace of mind.

The word went out that we would win the China Telecom deal. Our competitors had made all sorts of donations to the customer, including personal computer systems for their new offices. Others had promised . . . well, other things. But we could guarantee the cooperation of the phone company itself.

As the word spread that we had won China Telecom—long before we actually had won it, certainly months before we signed a contract—it influenced the award of the large project, the wiring of the Industrial and Commercial Bank of China (ICBC) headquarters. Our major competitor had ordered cases of champagne to celebrate their winning of the glamorous deal, but at the last moment it was my small company, brand new to the market, that seized the city by using the villages. The

ICBC people had heard that we were the winners of the smaller, China Telecom deal and that—coupled with our stellar performance in the technical aspect of the negotiations, mentioned in Chapter One—sealed the deal. We actually signed the contract for ICBC before we signed the one for China Telecom . . . and the decision-maker at China Telecom told us that we won their contract because of . . . you guessed it . . . ICBC.

> **Without preparedness, superiority is not real superiority and there can be no initiative either. Having grasped this point, a force which is inferior but prepared can often defeat a superior enemy by surprise attack.**
>
> **—Chairman Mao**

Taking the initiative, therefore, does not only mean attacking and staying in the customer's face. It also means thinking strategically and seizing smaller victories along the way. By winning the support of the man at the Beijing Phone Company—simply by showing up and being respectful of his power—that victory had won us another, that of China Telecom, which, in turn, won us the grand prize, ICBC. Further, by paying attention to the actual physical site of the installation itself and noting differences between the site and the blueprints—from which all our other competitors were working—we were able to demonstrate to the customer that we had the technical expertise necessary to carry through on our contract. Of course, ICBC was nervous. They did not know for sure that we would be able to successfully complete the project, but the overwhelming evidence we provided to them in terms of our understanding of Chinese business infrastructure and installation and engineering practices was too much to ignore. ICBC is now a showplace of modern, high-technology data and voice wiring, using both copper and fiber-optic-based networks. Photographs of our installation adorn their corporate brochures.

Give full play to our style of fighting—courage in battle, no fear of sacrifice, no fear of fatigue, and continuous fighting (that is, fighting successive battles in a short time without rest).

—Chairman Mao

What was not so obvious were the sleepless nights we spent in drafting the technical and commercial proposals, or the final pricing nightmare that took place in the wee hours of the morning on the day we were to present the sealed quote as Peter Wong and I debated how low we should go. To take the initiative in China you must be willing and able to work very long hours under very stressful and uncomfortable circumstances. In this particular case, we were in an unheated room in December of 1996, freezing our fingers off as we re-punched numbers into a cheap plastic calculator, estimating the final cost for the whole project and the price we could live with in clouds made by our breath in the darkness of a Beijing winter night, under the harsh glare of flickering fluorescent lights.

Our head office, upon hearing about the victory, cracked open their own bottles of champagne and celebrated. In less than a year, we had not only penetrated the China market but won the single most important project there. I understand the champagne flowed for a week back home. I didn't have any. I wasn't there. Instead Peter and I worked on our next projects and kept the momentum going, between meals of Mongolian hotpot and steins of Chinese beer at a small Beijing restaurant frequented only by locals, and by us at least two or three times a week. We nailed China Telecom, and then went on to quote Unicom and other utilities. We attacked projects in Szechuan Province, in Qingdao, in Anhui, in Wuxi, in Shanghai, in Urumqi. We signed up banks, insurance companies, construction outfits, computer firms. We kept the pressure up, now in one town, now in another. As the American vice president, my presence was necessary everywhere to demonstrate to our customers that, yes, this was truly an American company and yes, I was there to show that we were committed to each and every customer.

We held seminars everywhere, invited total strangers to lunch and dinner, collected thousands of name cards, and tried to keep everyone and their positions and their companies straight in our minds. This was hit-and-run tactics, and for a while I felt like Colonel Kurtz in *Apocalypse Now!*, going upriver, never stopping, fighting all the way to the Afghan border. There were days when I was not sure which province I was in, or which customers I was going to see. No matter. It would all eventually be revealed, so I sat back and reviewed my sales presentations and got ready for the flack.

In many cases, there will be people who are annoyed by your presence in the market. They have already built up relationships with your competitors and have benefited in some way. There might be corruption involved, not necessarily through your competitor directly but via a sales agent or some other, more shadowy figure. They might be angry simply because they have backed the wrong horse; now that you are the golden boy (or girl, as it may be) they look a little stupid or like yesterday's news. They will try to disrupt your progress, either by challenging you during one of your seminars (as has happened to me more than once) or by agitating against you behind your back (as has happened to me more times than I care to remember). They will use their own *guanxi* as leverage against you wherever they can. It has become a point of honor with them, and they will either give up right away due to lack of support from their colleagues . . . or they will wage a constant war of attrition, spreading rumors, lies, and innuendo about you and your company in the marketplace. When you realize that China is very sensitive to gossip-mongering, you will understand the potential seriousness of this problem.

I have been called everything you can imagine in China by my enemies. I have been accused of frequenting prostitutes, bribery and corruption, public drunkenness (well, okay, maybe *that* one . . .), and even being an agent for the CIA. With the exception of the latter, these are all charges that could be leveled against many Chinese executives themselves but which are somehow worse when applied to a foreigner.

How do you defend yourself against these charges, especially when they come at an early stage of your campaign? In the first place, you don't address the charges directly, as there is virtually no way to prove a negative and you will only look stupid in the process. The best thing you can do is to discover the source of the rumors and address it. If it is someone in your customer's company who is disgruntled because they switched to you instead of the competitor they had been working with, it is only necessary to approach that individual and try to come to terms with him or her. That does not mean bribery or any kind of illegal or unethical conduct; what it does mean is taking the person out to lunch or dinner and doing your best to bond. A show of respect for that individual will go a long way toward defusing the situation.

Remember: in this as in everything in China, *always* take the initiative. And *never* give up.

The Enemy

We should rid our ranks of all impotent thinking. All views that overestimate the strength of the enemy and underestimate the strength of the people are wrong.

— Chairman Mao

Initiative must not only come from you and your team in the field; it must also come from your superiors in the home office. The great value that you have as a smaller company fighting against larger competitors in a market as huge in terms of population, landmass, and potential earnings as China is your ability to make decisions swiftly and to react immediately to any external changes. Your competitor's strength is in its early presence in the market, its brand-name recognition, and the amount of resources it has at its disposal. Its weakness is its size and the burden it has of satisfying anonymous shareholders to whom it cannot make a case for further investment, and of dealing with a bureaucratic chain of command anytime it comes to a change of policy, direction, focus, or strategy. Your people must not be intimidated by the size and power of your competitor. The situation is not nearly as hopeless as it appears. In my decades in China trade I have always been able to take work away from much larger and better-known American, European, and Japanese companies by taking advantage of their weaknesses and by exploiting my company's strengths in just precisely this manner.

No Chinese company wants to give all its business to one company; it is not good strategic thinking. By giving all its business to your competitor it will increase its dependence on that company and become, in effect, its serf. The Chinese company would rather have options, and would be more comfortable in using products from a variety of sources; not a large variety, because that would be self-defeating in terms of spare parts, training, etc., but having two or three standard suppliers of the same type of equipment or service or product means that if one company fails to provide adequate support or competitive pricing, the company can always rely upon another. That is where you come in.

There will always be business in China for you, no matter how mature they tell you the market has become for your products. Some companies will fail to live up to their promises, made in the heat of passion over the first contract negotiation. Other companies will suffer from take-overs and buy-outs, changing personnel and policy and outsourcing their manufacturing and making the Chinese nervous in the process. You have to be on top of the situation there, ready at any moment to take the place of a competitor in a failing relationship with a Chinese client. There will be opportunity for this and you have to be ready to seize the initiative when it happens.

In addition, a large company often issues dictats to its overseas branches and operations that make no sense locally even though they seem eminently reasonable back home. For instance, they will demand that personnel stationed overseas be rotated back to the States—or wherever—after two years, thus confusing the hell out of the Chinese who have just gotten used to the first crop of executives. The amount of time, money, and tender, loving care it has taken to develop close ties with the Chinese clients is thrown out of the window overnight because a bureaucrat has created a human resources policy that makes no sense when it comes to the difficult and lucrative China market. The temptation to create a uniform corporate policy is almost overwhelming to a certain type of middle-level executive, and the negative repercussions of this type of action are incalculable . . . but they improve your chances immensely. Every time one of your competitors falls in love with its own image and tries to solidify its corporate structure it becomes inflexible and dictatorial, even toward its client base. There will come a time when a company's persona—or the CEO's ego—becomes more important than the customer it serves, and that is when smaller, more flexible and mobile companies seize market share away from them.

When a Bill Gates shows up in China, it is always a big event. Virtually every Chinese businessman or woman knows who he is, and knows about Microsoft. Is this an insuperable hurdle when it comes time to sell your own software package?

Microsoft, for all its presence in the world market, is not well-received in China for several reasons. In the first place, the Windows operating system and all its variants and revisions are too costly for a developing nation. One simply cannot charge in China, or Malaysia, or Indonesia the same price one would charge in New York or London for the same product, no matter what it is, if the goal is to seize market share. Pricing must be realistic. However, the high price of Microsoft products has put them out of reach of the average consumer, and this has led to piracy.

In the second place, Microsoft's operating system is not the most user-friendly in the world. It typically has so many patches and needs so much on-line updating that what may be merely frustrating for an American consumer is a disaster for an overseas operator in a country where Internet access is either tightly controlled by the government or simply too slow and erratic to be relied upon.

China, therefore, has seriously considered switching to an upstart: the Linux operating system, which is open-source, more efficient, and . . . most important . . . free. This has forced Microsoft to make all sorts of concessions to the Chinese market in order to protect itself, but the handwriting is on the wall. Microsoft will either have to change its sales policies or concede many overseas markets as independent software developers provide Linux-based programs that are less expensive than their Microsoft-based counterparts and easier to use. Microsoft's litigious nature has also made the Chinese uncomfortable in a society that values cooperation over confrontation.

You are in China to fulfill a need. As your larger, more powerful competitors begin to lose sight of their real purpose the Chinese will increasingly turn to newer, more efficient and more flexible companies. In addition, deals with Microsoft happen at a very high corporate and government level; smaller Chinese companies and middle-level managers do not have that kind of access to Bill Gates. They have access to you.

Another advantage you have over the larger enemy is your ability to listen to the people on the ground. A company like Microsoft pushes a single vision, a single identifiable product. That can be a strength in a developed country where product and image are inextricably bound together, to set the company apart from its competitors, but it is certainly a problem in a poorer country or among poorer consumers who cannot afford the luxury of a "vision" but need a solution, usually one that is tailored more to their immediate needs. Your direct access to the engineering and technical staff at your company means you can help provide solutions that are designed to "fit" the Chinese market, both in terms of application and cost. Everyone talks about the 1.2 billion consumers in China but no one actually *listens* to them. If you do, you will be in a position to steal serious share away from the giants.

> **Production by the masses, the interests of the masses, the experiences and feelings of the masses—to these the leading cadres should pay constant attention.**
>
> **—Chairman Mao**

For instance, China is capable of manufacturing a great many things. They have inundated world markets with inexpensive textiles and household goods, and a Chinese-made automobile will soon hit the market in the United States. Their problems lie in quality control generally and in some high-technology items which require strenuous quality control measures every step of the way. Often, Chinese firms lack the precision process control equipment that would make quality control issues easier to handle; more often, they simply lack the will. If they applied Western-style QC methods to their production lines they would have to reject more than 20 percent of their output, which means 20 percent waste. This is something Chinese factory directors feel they cannot afford to do, so they have been willing in the past to overlook many QC issues in favor of meeting quotas and deadlines and maintaining profitability. Of course, this sounds familiar to every Western factory director, too, but if factories in the West shipped substandard merchandise they would lose their customers. For most Chinese factories, their customers are local Chinese consumers who have been slow to complain. When it comes to export, however, the demand for quality control becomes paramount. There comes a point where an inexpensive product of poor quality is rejected in favor of a more expensive product with better quality.

You are in a position to help Chinese firms increase their access to foreign markets. Your own factory operates according to strict quality control measures (at least, I assume it does!), and that means QC on the raw materials coming in as well as on the finished product going out. You have technology to transfer you didn't know you had. By sharing this information on the QC process with a potential customer, you increase the value of the relationship. Further, you can help that customer by providing introductions to potential clients in your own country or anywhere else your company has operations and distribution channels. Many of your larger competitors wouldn't even think of this angle because it is not directly related to their sales targets. We are talking about market share, though, and not this quarter's sales figures. Your competitors need to show growth every month or else their sales managers lose their jobs; you need to take a more long-term approach and slowly build up a customer base that is unshakeable because you have made yourself indispensable.

You can also take advantage of China's huge manufacturing base to source some of your components locally. This way you reduce landed costs and, in the process, build more relationships among the "masses." Of course, the core elements of your production must be imported from abroad—at least until you have created a strong reputation for quality and can afford to start manufacturing some of your essential product line in China. For now, though, China provides excellent opportunities for light assembly and some production, such as plastic molding, metal stamping, etc. Further, if your business sells prepackaged components or parts of any kind it makes more sense to ship in bulk to China and have a local operation do the repackaging. You would save money on the materials and labor in your home country, as well as shipping costs which would be reduced if you ship in bulk rather than in packaged lots. This increases your profitability and allows you to be more competitive.

Further, by using China as a light assembly or packaging base in Asia you are in a better position to attack other markets in the region, such as Singapore, Malaysia, Thailand, Indonesia, and other Southeast Asian countries.

Your lead times would be shorter and your shipping costs cheaper. In addition, there is a large interlocking network of Chinese businesspeople across Asia with connections (*guanxi*!) in various vertical market segments. While based in Kuala Lumpur, I had colleagues with good relationships in freight forwarding, manufacturing, assembly, packaging, advertising, and printing throughout China, Hong Kong, and Southeast Asia. These relationships meant cost savings to my company as well as increased sales. You don't have to be a multibillion dollar corporation to have such an infrastructure at your fingertips. Companies grossing less than fifty million dollars a year have been able to create such an assembly, manufacturing, and marketing platform in Asia. You could do it no matter the size of your company, because there is no upfront cost to you beyond travel, entertainment, and communications. Many Chinese companies are eager to work with foreign firms in this manner, and they advertise in the trades and through the Internet. As long as their responsibilities are for non-critical products and services—unless you are absolutely certain of their quality control practices and the acceptability to the market of having a local manufacturer—you should experience no serious problems in using such companies in a support capacity. And . . . having this kind of infrastructure up and running makes you look like one of your major competitors. Eventually, this approach will become solidified to the point where you *are* one of the major competitors.

Mao understood what he was up against. He knew he could not fight a pitched battle against the enemy; he just did not have the resources. Instead, his approach to battle re-imagined the battlefield, enabling him to fight a different kind of war. By changing the rules, he managed to outwit the enemy who was playing by the old rules. He concentrated on the "masses," which means the people on the ground whose lives would be changed forever by the outcome of the war. He relied on a different form of propaganda, one based not only on Communist theory—that would have been a tough sell—but one based on identifying the needs of the consumers (sorry, I mean, the "masses") and speaking to those needs. He elevated the dialogue above that of nationalist pride and changed it into a question of the ownership of the means of production: something every villager could get behind.

Your enemy often does not understand that. They have a product they want to sell, at a price structure that works at home. They try to convince the "masses" that their product is of the best quality, which only makes the average Chinese consumer laugh because everyone says the same thing. It's an outside-in approach: the company comes into the country, selling a product that has already sold well in Holland or Hoboken, as-is. You, on the other hand, are not your product. You are the brains and the brawn that created that product. You are the technology behind it. You are the creative force that produced the product, and could produce another. You have to take the inside-in approach and understand the needs of the people—of your market—and find out how to re-imagine your product line for local consumption. Your competitor is too large for that; they can't dedicate a special team to creating a version of their product "just" for the Chinese market. It would take too much time, require too many approvals, take months to get up to speed, and they would probably still get it wrong! You can do all of that much faster and much more cheaply . . . and with a lot more intelligence.

This does not require re-tooling your entire firm. You will be able to exploit your existing investment in machinery and tooling for the most part. There will be changes, however. Metric versus English, for instance. Different electrics. Chinese language instructions. Increased protection against environmental factors. Some of this can be solved by sourcing some components locally, in China itself. Other changes are not that dire or expensive. But the goodwill and trust of your new customer base is invaluable and worth the effort. And, one side benefit to all of this is that you will be able to deploy the same product changes in other foreign markets that use the same electrics, the same metric system, and the same environmental requirements. By becoming involved in China trade, your whole company will change and will become a global player virtually overnight.

In my previous incarnation as a vice president for international trade my focus on China enabled us to penetrate other foreign markets, particularly in Europe. Our increased profile got the attention of major players in Italy, France, and the UK and eventually resulted in an offer to buy our company from a French electronics giant. In addition, our China experience enabled us to help one of our American distributors in South America that was involved in business negotiations with a Chinese mining firm. This resulted in increased business for us in South America, both with our American distributor and the Chinese. The possibilities for you are truly endless. You just have to throw away the "box" and think like a Chinese businessperson who will never leave an opportunity lying on the table but who will take the time to think about how she can leverage a casual acquaintance or some gossip about another project or another company into some new business. As mentioned above, you must always take the initiative and be open to new ways of re-inventing your China business as new opportunities present themselves. It is the best way of fighting the enemy, and of using the villages to encircle the city. You have a "liberty of action" that the larger firms don't have; they are hamstrung by all sorts of issues and concerns, many of them invented by zealous employees interested more in keeping their jobs than in building the business. The initiative is yours.

Chapter 7
The Seventh Stratagem

Whoever wants to know a thing has no way of doing so except by coming into contact with it, that is, by living in its environment.

—Chairman Mao

Ain't that the truth?

All the books you have been reading about China and business—including this one—do not completely prepare you for the experience of being *in* China. There is a corollary to this, and that is your people back home cannot hope to understand what it is you are up against and what it is necessary to do in order to accomplish great things here. Your eyes have been opened by being in China for a few weeks . . . or months . . . or, in my case, more than twenty years. And you're still not an expert. Imagine the shipping department. Accounting. Engineering. All they have are parts of the elephant; they can't see the whole animal from where they stand. They are relying on you for the complete picture.

China is not simply another market, like Idaho or Kansas City or even Barcelona or Buenos Aires. Every market has its particular quirks and subtle obstacles, but China is another case altogether. Personally, I have a hard time selling in Middle America, and particularly in the South where I am considered the worst of all possible Yankees: a New Yorker. A New Yorker is not even a real American, according to most people I meet. (It was only in the immediate days and weeks after 9/11 that New Yorkers felt like they were part of the United States, when other Americans rallied around them. That bonding was short-lived, however!) Yet, in China, I am suddenly American.

This sets up a barrier between you and your customers, just as it would anywhere else you are a stranger. It is up to you to break down the barrier, but not lose your identity in the process. You will never be accepted as another Chinese, no matter how hard you try, so don't try. You can, however, meet them halfway and adopt their business etiquette and respect their cultural values. I don't mean you have to go all Alan Alda (or Richard Gere) on them, but only that you recognize that one catches more flies with honey than with vinegar. You also have to remember that you are in a Communist country, regardless of the neon lights and the karaoke bars. The Party controls the economic development of the country, and it has representatives everywhere: in every town and village, in every factory and government office or agency. That means that the business environment is a little different from one you would find anywhere else.

> **In China, the struggle to consolidate the socialist system, the struggle to decide whether socialism or capitalism will prevail, will take a long historical period.**
>
> **—Chairman Mao**

There is an uneasy relationship between the burgeoning capitalist economy of China and its historical context, not only of Chairman Mao and the Communist Party but also of centuries of exploitation by foreigners. You are one of those foreigners. It's a new day, to be sure, and we are talking about New China . . . but nonetheless there is suspicion and distrust, mixed with a kind of weird fascination with everything Western. There is even, now, a new cultural trend:

Maoist chic.

Everywhere in China, but especially in the cities, young people who never knew the real Mao have adopted Mao fashions, are singing songs with lyrics based on the *Little Red Book*, and are going to restaurants decorated with photographs of the Chairman. Mao has become strangely fashionable lately, and this may contribute to a revaluation of his life and work. No one is starry-eyed about the Great Leader, however. They recognize the horrible suffering his policies created, particularly in the 1950s with the Great Leap Forward and other draconian—almost surreal—measures undertaken to protect and strengthen the country but which led instead to the deaths of millions by starvation and the pain caused to many millions more. The excesses of the Cultural Revolution in the 1960s contributed to much of the cynicism of people in their forties and fifties and sixties, when the intelligentsia were sent to the countryside to work the fields, separated from their families, sometimes forever. Patriotic Chinese were abused, tortured, and humiliated because they had a foreign friend, or there was a foreign language book in their house, or simply because they were suspected of counter-revolutionary tendencies.

With all of that, however, there has been a resurgence of interest where the Chairman is concerned. He is a fact they cannot avoid, the eight-hundred-pound gorilla in the closet. He gave them their country, their freedom, their pride; and in many cases killed them, tortured them, and starved them in the process. If there is a kind of revisionism taking place among the young, it is probably nothing more than a passing fad: one that will eventually be replaced by a more sober reappraisal of Mao's legacy.

However that shakes out, you will be going to China at a turbulent time in that country's history. There is a kind of revolt taking place in the countryside among the farmers and peasants who had formed the core of Mao's revolution. They are dissatisfied with the way the people in the cities are doing so much better than they are; they are angry at being considered bumpkins and backward; and they want their respect and their piece of the pie, too. They are moving to the cities in ever larger numbers, straining the ability of the municipalities to cope with the additional stress of hundreds of thousands of new residents on an already barely functioning infrastructure. Many parts of Beijing, Shanghai, and other cosmopolitan centers still do not have indoor plumbing or adequate heat, electricity, and other utilities, and the strain of accommodating millions of new residents is enormous. In addition, the rural newcomers are cheated of their wages in many cases and forced to work construction jobs that pay little in the first place. Back home, they are faced with a spectacle that would make Mao roll over in his mausoleum: farmland being bought up by investors and turned into American-style housing developments, with homes in the one million dollar price range. The farmers who worked that land often get none of the money, and the decision to sell is usually made without their knowledge or approval.

There are today roughly seven hundred million Chinese in the countryside, with another five hundred million or more in the cities. Can you grasp the enormity of the situation? The latest US census has three hundred million living in the entire United States of America. The number of people living in China's cities *alone* is nearly twice that. One cannot help wondering if the dislocations taking place in China's economy and society are due not so much to the incompetence of its leadership, but to the sheer impossibility of effectively managing a population that huge. India, which has a population approaching the size of China's, is experiencing some of the same growth pains but is not growing quite so explosively as China and China has none of India's religious diversity as an added factor. China is a country without religion. It is a nation that has grown up not knowing what goes on inside a church or a temple. It is a nation whose values are based not on the Ten

Commandments or the Dhammapada or the Qur'an, but on the *Quotations* of Chairman Mao.

Many writers insist that Confucianism and Daoism are an essential part of China's collective psyche and that to understand China and to be successful there you have to be familiar with these ideas. Perhaps. But how many Chinese today have read the *Dao De Jing*, for instance, or the Confucian *Book of Rites*? About as many as have read the Bible, I would imagine; on my first trip to China in 1986 no one could identify Lao Tzu—the author of the *Dao De Jing*—or understand the symbolism of the yin-yang emblem. No one had ever cast the *I Jing*, or "worshipped" their ancestors. And when I took Chinese delegations to the States, they would be confused about the purpose of churches and temples. They would only relax when they were able to characterize them as "meeting halls." This means that when you are in China you are confronting a profound difference in the way people approach life, meaning, and values. I am not making any judgments here, by the way. I am not saying that the Chinese value system is inherently inferior or superior to ours. But it is different.

On top of that, you should also be aware of how the Chinese government handles political dissidents. Harshly. They are kept under surveillance (when they are not in prison) and their phones are tapped and they are followed wherever they go. Unauthorized religious groups—like Falun Gong—are routinely characterized as "cults" and their members rounded up and imprisoned. Authorized religions do not fare that much better, even though their memberships may be tiny by any standards. The Chinese government arrogates to itself who can become a bishop or a cardinal in the local Catholic Church, thus effectively removing it from Vatican control. They have done the same to the Tibetan religion, deciding who can and can't become the Panchen Lama, for example; once the Dalai Lama dies, they will decide who the next one will be and that will cause tremendous disruption among the Tibetan population still living in China.

In broad strokes, this is the China you will be visiting. Rampant capitalism on the one hand, totalitarian dictatorship on the other. When I speak with Chinese anywhere in China, the feelings are expressed pretty much the same: they are interested in improving their lives, making money, getting better living conditions, and going abroad. This is especially true of the young, who, as university students, are clamoring for positions in overseas colleges.

The Cultural Revolution started forty years ago, in 1966. Mao died thirty years ago, in 1976. These anniversaries passed pretty quietly. But the effects of both have been deep, and analysis of Mao's legacy is patchy, halting, and unsure. To the young, he is no longer a person but a kind of god. The father of the country. The man who brought China out of the dark ages and into its rightful position as a world superpower. To the older generation, he is the dominant figure of their past, for good or for ill.

When you go to China—when you have found an agent, identified a project, and are eager to get underway and make a difference—you will meet both these types of Chinese: the young students who will work as your interpreters, or as employees—engineers, technicians—of the businesses you are approaching, all bright and shiny and eager to make your acquaintance; and the older Chinese with the experience of generations of suffering in their eyes, cynical perhaps, realistic certainly, who will listen politely to your spiel but who will occasionally stare off into the middle distance of the Middle Kingdom, watching another tragedy unfold in the dark corners of their memory. They may have been cadres, Red Guards, during the Cultural Revolution who oversaw the brutalization of their professors, their bosses, their neighbors . . . or they may have been the ones who lost their family, their friends . . . their pride, surrounded by shouting teenagers waving the *Little Red Book* as they were made to publicly confess their sins in endless self-criticism sessions in the re-education camps. You need to know this, because the occasional bitterness, anger, disinterest, cynicism, sadness, and reproach you will see in some of the older faces around the conference table have nothing at all to do with you, but with history.

> **A revolution is not a dinner party, or writing an essay, or painting a picture, or doing embroidery; it cannot be so refined, so leisurely and gentle, so temperate, kind, courteous, restrained and magnanimous.**
>
> **—Chairman Mao**

All that aside, there are a number of other things to be aware of when you travel in China. We have already discussed such niceties as the business banquet, business etiquette, etc., but there are other issues we must address for your own personal comfort and well-being.

First and foremost: don't drink the water. The Chinese don't, and neither should you. Tap water is normally contaminated in China and can infect you with all sorts of parasites. Drink only boiled water. The Chinese have a habit of sipping cups of very hot, almost scalding, water every day for health reasons. Sometimes with a few limp and unimpressive tea leaves languishing at the bottom. Drink bottled water if you have to (be careful and check the cap to make sure it has not been opened and refilled), or better yet, stick to canned soft drinks or beer. When you brush your teeth, use bottled water or boiled water; both of these are usually present in your hotel room. Use them! When you take a shower, keep your mouth and other potential orifices closed tight against the spray. You will thank me for this advice later!

You will also notice that the Chinese generally do not eat fresh garden salads. There is a reason for that, too. Unless you are dining in one of the expensive Western hotels, you are not likely to see salad greens anywhere near you. That is because fruits and vegetables are grown in China using human waste as fertilizer. Therefore, eat only fruit you can peel first—such as oranges, bananas, etc.—and only vegetables that have been cooked. If you're washing your fruit or vegetables, remember what I said about the water in China. Use only boiled water or bottled water you feel safe with.

Restaurants are also a matter of some concern. Some foreigners eat at the street stalls and suffer no ill effects; it depends on what you eat and with what utensils. Chopsticks and bowls that have been washed in lukewarm water or dirty water are not safe, for all the obvious reasons. In restaurants it is not unusual to see Chinese wipe the chopsticks with their napkins or dip them in boiling water, just to make sure. The proliferation of disposable chopsticks has ameliorated this problem somewhat, but at the cost of a couple of forests full of trees.

If you must eat at a Western restaurant, you will find plenty of them in the major metropolitan areas. There are even Hard Rock Cafés in Beijing, Shanghai, and elsewhere that cater to a mixed foreign and local crowd. There are pubs aplenty now; in the 1980s, there were none.

The cities are relatively safe, but crime is on the increase.

A case in point:

China can be a dangerous place to do business for a foreigner. There are cultural norms that can be transgressed, offensive actions innocently committed, people unnecessarily insulted. The water can kill you, and so can the endless negotiations that you have no hope of winning but participate in anyway for the sake of "face." And there are other dangers.

During the installation phase of the famous ICBC project mentioned several times in these pages, we had three or four engineers over from the States to supervise the work. One of these was an ethnic Chinese, born in Hong Kong but raised in the United States and a US citizen. He spoke Mandarin and Cantonese fluently, and for that reason was an invaluable member of our installation team.

Several months into the hotly contested project, he received a phone call in his hotel room. Uncharacteristically, he left his room with the light on and his computer still running. Security cameras filmed him going down the hallway from his room and taking the elevator to the lobby of the hotel. More security cameras followed him through the lobby and out the doors. He was dressed casually, as if he was leaving the room for only a few minutes.

He left forever.

I received the phone call a few hours later. He had been attacked and was found on the street, his cell phone missing. In his delirium, he was speaking Cantonese. No one understood him. He was pronounced dead on arrival at the local hospital. He had been murdered.

The police launched an investigation, and they focused on our office and staff. There were rumors that this was an inside job, maybe a quarrel with one of the other installers or with someone else working for us. This was a typical reaction to the situation, for it would have been much easier for the Chinese to pin the blame on another foreigner. However, that end of the investigation got nowhere.

Another rumor had it that there had been a contract put out on him by people who were angry that we had won the project. Since he was Chinese, and spoke Mandarin fluently, he was sure to be a tremendous asset to our installation—which was exactly what the opposition did not want. They wanted us to fall flat on our faces. So, they killed him. That was the other rumor.

More likely he was the victim of some kind of confidence game. The call to his room has never been identified. The whereabouts of his cell phone have never been determined. The case has never been solved. It is possible that he felt overconfident in China—a country to which he had never been before—due to his ethnicity and his proficiency in the languages. Someone may have prevailed upon him in some way; asked for a loan, perhaps, or some other assistance, and lured him away from his hotel to be robbed. He died only a few yards from the hotel, so the circumstances are puzzling, to say the least.

What does this have to do with you?

You may feel comfortable after a while in China, but you are still a foreigner and a target for some unscrupulous types. Even our Chinese engineer was considered a foreigner, an "ABC" or "American Born Chinese." His clothes gave him away. His attitude. The way he walked or talked. Any of these things would have made him as a foreigner. So much more so a non-Chinese in China.

You are always in danger of being "adopted" by someone in the country. This could be be total stranger or someone you meet in a store or on the street. This person will speak to you in English, perhaps broken English, and try to start up a conversation with the "foreign friend." They will seem harmless, and often they are. Sometimes, though, there is a hidden agenda.

Your temptation to connect with the people can be very great. It's quite natural, and for some Americans in particular who seem so eager to be liked everywhere they go it's almost an addiction; and like any addiction, it can be dangerous to your health. Treat everyone you meet with kindness and politely, but don't feel obligated to respond to every overture of friendship, or invitations to coffee, or offers of informal tour guide, etc. This happens a lot in China, and sometimes it is quite innocent while at other times it is part of a kind of confidence game. Sometimes, it's a combination of the two, with a person seeing an opportunity and acting upon it.

I'm not trying to frighten anyone. If you are in the care of your sales agent, these things will not become issues and you will travel quite freely and without mishap because your agent knows the ropes and because those who mean you harm will avoid you once they notice your relationship with the local Chinese agent. If you are wandering around the streets on your own, though—and this is one of my favorite pastimes in China—then you increase the chance that someone will come up to you and start speaking a few words of English to gauge your reaction.

You can always pretend to be French.

The more time you spend observing your environment, the more you will realize how appropriate—or not—your product offering is in that country. Things that you take for granted—reliable electrical power, indoor plumbing, fast Internet service, landline phones—may not exist at all, or exist only sporadically. These environmental issues will impact the desirability of your offering. They will also give you ideas for new products, or ways to market your existing product lines.

When I was taking the German delegation from Beijing to Baoding, they noticed with intense interest the tarring of a roof on an old brick building in the middle of a field. Since that was their business—the manufacture of modified bitumen roofing material—they began to realize that the market was really based on a very primitive technology. The methods being used were those that had not been in common practice in Europe any time in the twentieth century. It was an education for them, and it took place only hours before our negotiation was to begin. It enabled them to modify their remarks to take into consideration the existing construction standards, and they were able to represent themselves as people who understood the local technology.

Also, modified bitumen is a petroleum-based product. The efficient operation of the plant they proposed needed a steady supply of a petroleum by-product. There was a refinery very close to where the factory would be erected, which would conceivably provide precisely the raw materials they needed. However, there was a problem.

According to the factory engineers, the raw material could only be provided in a solid form, not a liquid. This mystified the Germans. It meant that the refinery would solidify the raw material and ship it to the factory where it would then be re-liquified: a number of unnecessary processes that would increase cost, increase time, and perhaps even provide a less-than-optimum product with all the intermediate steps potentially contaminating the materials.

Eventually, we discovered why. The refinery routinely solidified the materials to make it easier for shipping long distances. In block form, it took up less space in the trucks than it would in liquid, bottled form and, anyway, they didn't have a lot of bottles.

In order to solve this problem, the Germans proposed that they speak to the refinery directly. This was embarrassing to the Chinese factory engineers, of course, who felt that the Germans saw them as incompetent. We were told again and again that "This is China. We have our own ways of doing things." That was all well and good, but it was not going to solve the problem of raw materials for a very expensive imported German production line for the manufacture of state-of-the-art roofing materials that they needed for the modern hotels and office buildings that were being erected all over the country.

What eventually transpired was typical for this type of negotiation in China. Someone on the staff of the Chinese factory knew someone on the staff at the refinery. The situation of transporting solid blocks of raw petroleum by-product was due to a policy that had been in place for more than a decade. The refinery could ship the raw materials in liquid form; it's just that no one had asked them before. The Chinese had gone on the assumption that the method that already existed—"we have always done it this way"—was the only one available to them. Up to this point in time, it had not been a problem so no one knew any better.

The change in process had taken place completely behind the scenes. We were simply told one day, without further comment, that they could now ship the raw material in liquid form. The Germans were happy. The Chinese were happy. I was intrigued, and finally got the story from Anthony Chang who got it from his contact in Baoding who got it from someone at the factory.

The modified bitumen plant contract was signed more than twenty years ago, in 1987. I worked day and night, literally, on the negotiations and the contract for weeks, perspiring in the heat of the Baoding Guest House and translating from the German specifications into English so that the English could be translated into Mandarin. It was thirsty work, and the Baoding Guest

House at that time did not have very much cold beer in stock due to their small refrigerator; so the Germans developed a system for keeping beer cold in their rooms: they simply stacked the cans, one atop the other, in columns in front of the rattling air conditioner. The ones directly in front of the air conditioner were cold, the others were warm. They pulled out the cold ones as desired (which was often), and rotated the others into position. That "art of German engineering" went on for weeks, but it preserved our sanity. In the end, that single successful negotiation spawned another half-dozen such projects in China, making the German company very pleased with the results of their total immersion course in China trade.

Interpreting what you see is important. You can jump to too many conclusions based on your own previous experience and knowledge. There is usually a perfectly logical explanation for a lot of the odd behavior you will notice in foreign lands, and China is perhaps the ultimate example of this; but if you don't have the cultural context, you are apt to make value judgments that are inappropriate and self-defeating.

That is where your sales agent comes in. His or her function is to interpret what you see for you, and to calm you down when you are in danger of losing your mind. In my case, that agent is Peter Wong.

Peter and I go back a long way, to a joint-venture negotiation between Shanghai Volkswagen and an American tire company in 1992. Since that time, we have been through many a brutally tough business deal, working together on three continents. Peter's background is classic: of Chinese descent, born in Saigon, university in Austria, residence in Canada, with a lovely wife from Beijing and two frighteningly smart children. He speaks several Chinese languages fluently (including Mandarin and Cantonese), as well as German and English. Like Anthony Chang, my old boss, before him Peter's knowledge of the intricate details of high-technology is not his forte; his specialty is getting the job done.

He knows that when a local engineer appears to be hostile to us, asking many unnecessary questions during a technical negotiation and raising a lot of rather silly issues, he is really on our side and is only doing all that to appear impartial to his colleagues.

He knows that when an American engineer shows up in Beijing and attempts to create a cubicle-like office environment for our staff—so common in America where we value our privacy—that it will be a disaster for the company, because that additional privacy means a lack of oversight and accountability, with some staff members cutting outside deals in their "cones of invisibility," unable to resist the temptation.

He knows that when a factory director politely declines our offer of dinner that evening, it means we have already lost the deal.

More important, though, Peter knows where the jobs are and who has the money to pay for them. His vast network of contacts (his *guanxi*) in so many different fields and industries in China is legendary. In addition, he can organize a seminar for a hundred people at the drop of a hat, get Chinese language brochures printed in a week, and arrange for travel all over China to chase jobs that we hear about on the grapevine.

My memories of Peter Wong are many and varied. There have been times we have stayed up all night drinking tall, liter-size bottles of beer until the wee hours of the morning, strategizing, plotting, planning, munching on stir-fried anchovies or boiled peanuts as we drew figures and calculated costs on napkins, business cards, coasters, receipts, only to stagger outside on a cold Beijing winter's night and wonder how we are getting back to our respective homes.

There were other times when we hosted American delegations—our employers, our engineers, our trade partners—in China, introducing them to the peculiarities of doing business in a Communist country, in Asia, wincing every time one of them said or did something stupid or ill-mannered and patching it over with the local com-

pany. Often, the older executives we brought over had
baggage of their own where China was concerned, lega-
cies of the Korean War, the Cold War, and decades of the
"Yellow Peril." They arrived in Beijing with chips on their
shoulders, politics mixed with ethnophobia and the kind
of Rosie O'Donnell racism that characterizes Chinese
people and their culture as silly and inferior, a combination of "no tickee no washee" laundry shop clichés and
the stereotype of Asians as some kind of miniature
Munchkin race in a land remarkably like Oz. The obverse
of that is the glorification of China and Chinese culture as
inherently superior: the "inscrutable" Chinese with their
acupuncture, their kung fu and t'ai chi, their exotic cuisine, and their mastery of the mystic arts. Somewhere in
there is the glamorization of the Chinese female and her
characterization as docile, submissive, erotic, and sensu-
ous: more mystery, wrapped in the promise of pleasure,
like those fat, deep-fried egg rolls in "Chinese" restaurants in the States that Americans mistakenly believe are
staples of the Chinese diet.

There were times, though, when Wong and I performed miracles in China, and against incredible odds.
Some of that was luck; most of it was hard work; and a little of it was *guanxi* and common sense. When Mao
instructed his troops during the Revolution, he told them
how important it was to master the terrain, to know the
people living there, to learn from them, and to truly live off
the land. Living off the land does not mean merely eating
what is available in its fields and forests, but identifying
with the land, understanding it, coming to terms with it,
making it your own.

A Chinese saying is appropriate here: to know a thing,
you must know what it eats. What the Chinese eat—what
they take in, ingest, consume, even believe—is a key to
their identity and a clue to the seemingly ephemeral
nature of its marketplace. The Chinese say they eat anything that flies, swims, crawls, or walks. I can personally
assure you that this is true. In the West, we are far more
selective, far more picky. We would normally not dream of

eating snakes, scorpions, or sea cucumbers. "What am I eating?" is one of the most frequent questions a foreigner asks in China, regardless of the dish's elegant appearance or exquisite taste. We segregate raw materials from each other, deciding which is edible and which is not. Like the Biblical injunctions we inherited from our own culture— the kosher laws prohibiting the consumption of pork or fish without scales—we decide first what is permitted and what is not.

The Chinese have had no such luxury, or they would have starved to death. Instead, what epitomizes the Chinese approach to food is the art in which everything and anything is prepared. This is a key to unlocking the door of "inscrutability": you take what you have to work with and make it palatable. Nothing is off-limits. Nothing is forbidden. Only the manner of using, making, working, eating . . . this is the stuff of art that enables the Chinese to not only survive but excel. What is forbidden is bad taste, poor etiquette, a lousy chef, an incompetent engineer; but even then, the Chinese will try to find a way to compromise, to cooperate, to collaborate in such a way that the desired result is achieved. The raw materials are not as important, not as crucial, as the process that transforms them into something useful, something edible.

Process is the essential factor. On a bright autumn afternoon in 1988, I saw a man in Beijing walk down the street with a handful of wet noodles. Literally. No bag, no container, no bowl. He had his noodles in a slithery lump in his hand and he was smiling. The process was working: he was transporting his lunch. The end result was assured: he would eat his lunch. What else was there to say?

Anything can be eaten, if prepared properly. Anything can be believed, if presented properly. Our advertising executives, our intelligence agencies, and our political leaders have known this secret for decades. It has a corollary: if enough people believe something, it becomes truth.

Your product, your company, your reputation, your capabilities, your technology: all of it is marketable in China as it is elsewhere. It's just a question of understanding

China's environment and preparing the meal in the most attractive, most delicious manner of which you are capable. And if your meal must be eaten with a fork and knife back home, it would be better if one could use chopsticks in China. The hard work—the cutting, the marinating, the stir-frying—is done by the chef, not the consumer. Do your homework, investigate the terrain, speak with the people . . . and when your dish is ready it will be embraced by a population hungry for new sensations.

Chapter 8
The Eighth Stratagem

Weapons are an important factor in war, but not the decisive factor; it is people, not things, that are decisive.

—Chairman Mao

Finally, we have to address the central issue of any business: people. There are those that are your customers and trade partners, and there are those who work for you and with you. In the end, it all comes down to human beings and not products or technology. The way you understand and manage people—and their needs and desires—is indicative of how successful you will be. Unfortunately, people are very different and the strategies you use in one market will not be workable in another and this goes for both your customers and your staff.

We have spent a lot of time discussing cultural and environmental factors in approaching China trade. We've talked about your "weapons": your sales, marketing, and technical strategies and tactics, your knowledge and use of Chinese business etiquette, the importance of adapting to local customs and traditions. All of this has to do with people, of course, but now we will focus on the Chinese people themselves.

It is always a mistake to generalize about any nation or any race. With China, however, we are faced with more internal diversity than you will find in any other country. The nation is a conglomeration of different languages, ethnic groups, cultures, customs, and, before the Revolution, different religions and political structures as well. How, then, to begin to understand the people who make up that virtual reality we call China?

The Chinese will not expect you to be able to tell the difference between a native of Guangdong (Canton) Province and one from Hebei or Jiangsu. They won't expect you to be able to speak any more Mandarin than *ni hao* ("How are you?"). And they will smile appreciatively as you struggle your way through a meal using chopsticks. But why live *down* to their expectations? There are issues deeper than the ones we have been discussing so far, and rather than give you some pat answers or formulaic concepts to memorize I thought I would quote from my China notebooks going back a number of years. In this way, you can understand what motivates the people you will meet and what keeps some of them from welcoming you with open arms.

August 30, 1986   Baoding Guest House   7:56 pm

Watching TV commercials for consumer products (some of which I can't identify) . . . I hear "Girls Just Want to Have Fun" as background music for an ad for washing machines. I wonder who chooses their music.

The day began at 8:00 am with breakfast. Just AC [Anthony Chang]'s brother and myself. Questions about where I live, how much my apartment costs. How many children I have.

At 8:50 am or so, my first meeting. This with the Baoding Relay Factory. They want to buy technology. As I finished with them, the hosiery machine people returned, and then a group wanting a system to design transformers, and then a group wanting a power control system and then lunch with the latter two groups. Then discussions with the latter two groups. Then the frequency changer people and then dinner. Five different projects. Seven meetings. Nothing much resolved at any of them but we leave Baoding tomorrow.

AC's brother is a living example of the last forty years of Chinese history.

He studied electrical engineering in school, and English. Then the Japanese invasion and he was forced to study Japanese. Then the end of the war and back to English. Then Russian, while English was forcibly abandoned. Then the Russians fell out of favor. The Cultural Revolution, and he was sent to the countryside to work as a peasant for over ten years, then rehabilitation, and with it back to English. He regrets deeply the lengthy hiatus from his studies and his work. He told me, "It is a very sad story."

He had a classmate, a young woman who was never very bright. She escaped to the West and eventually became a professor at an American university. Recently, she came back to China as a well-respected specialist and expert. He told the story without much emotion, but in his place I would feel extreme rage. This is the land of Kafka . . .

Mr. Yun is the money man. He attends all meetings that have to do with Baoding. He seems to speak some English, but then they all do. He is accompanied by an older man, thin, nervous, who chain-smokes and moves restlessly into and out of meetings with urgent phone messages for Mr. Yun. He appears to be the victim of some previous purge or other and too many criticism sessions. His anger is palpable, a chronic state like his nervousness or his nicotine addiction.

AC's brother, however, has the ready smile but slightly apprehensive or frightened look of someone who has also faced many criticism sessions, but who has somehow survived by being nice. Anthony told me how he escaped torture by finding out the right cadre to bribe.

Yun, on the other hand, wears a black leather jacket and black horn-rims, looks vaguely Western, rides a motorcycle—an anomaly around here—and acts slightly aloof. He controls the money: who gets what, how much, and for which project. The others defer to him. He generally stays out of discussions, but when he talks, they listen. At the dinner with the mayor last night he sat on the left side, AC at the right.

August 31, 1986   Room 7006, Beijing Hotel, Beijing   10:25 pm

Lunch at a restaurant in Baoding with Yun, his gofer, Anthony, his brother, myself, and Mr. Guo and the Relay people. Turtle meat. Turtle soup. Many dumplings. Warm beer. A few toasts. Back in the car for Beijing, my stomach sending signals. Get out at the Baoding Guest House to use the restroom (the one at the restaurant was a tile ditch for urinating, and nothing else; I should probably describe the restaurant in more detail—the cracked and filthy linoleum floor, the folding chairs that kept collapsing, the heat, the stench from the faulty sewer system, the faded institutional green paint—but I won't). Went back to my room for a few moments. Worried about the 21/2–3 hour road trip to Beijing in my condition, but somehow we make it.

We had checked out of the hotel at 11:30 am and drove—suitcases and all—to the restaurant. Thousands of people on the streets in the heat (it's at least 32 degrees C), riding bicycles or walking. The people I see are pure campesinos, and the countryside could be Colombia or parts of Chile. Even many of the people could pass for South Americans. Replace the Chinese signs with Spanish ones, and it would be hard to tell the difference.

There was a detour on the road to Beijing, so our trip took longer than expected. We arrived at the Beijing Hotel at 5:30 pm. Me: exhausted, ill with stomach twinges signaling a bout of diarrhea. Met at the hotel by Mo Ping's parents. AC's brother lives in an apartment building not far from the hotel and he repairs there.

AC's knock on the door at a quarter to six: dinner at 6:30 with Vice-Minister Li. Can I make it? Sick, tired, in need of a hot shower and bed, I say, "Sure. No problem." How can I miss this? One of the most powerful men in the country. An intimate dinner for seven.

Promptly at 6:30 we are met by a Mr. Yao. I do not know his function. He wears the typical Chinese summer outfit of white shirt over gray trousers, only this time topped by a porkpie hat. He leads us to a waiting car (not a taxi) which takes us to the Bian Yi Fang Roast Duck Restaurant, a reasonably elegant affair. We are on the second floor, but must climb what seem like four flights of stairs. The rooms are small, air conditioned, clean, and luxurious by China standards.

Minister Li arrives, accompanied by two men: one is a Commissioner of something and the other, a Western-looking man in a tie, is some assistant to the Minister. Their authority and importance for us lie mainly in the cable projects. Li greets Anthony like an old buddy and they chew the fat for awhile. Li apologizes for Shenzhen and Baoding, tells me not to judge China by those poor examples. I tell him I have been impressed by everything I have seen. (They laugh.) Li tells me I must come more often. I tell him I would like to. "Even to Baoding?" asks Anthony.

Dinner breaks up around 9:30. AC and I leave the others in the room, no doubt to discuss matters of state . . .

AC tells me the upshot is there is competition on the cables. Fierce competition from, of all places, Singapore. There will be a bloodbath of fierce negotiations on this project.

Tomorrow: dinner with the Post and Telecommunications Minister. (Not the Vice-Minister, the Minister.) Until then, rest in my room, relax . . . and draft a telex to Julia on the textile machines.

Outside my window there is a terrace. I can look out over the Imperial Palace, whose roofs seem to rise above the haze and mist, orange and graceful like boats gliding on a cloud.

There was thunder and lightning during dinner. A sudden rainfall, and the city is cooler. I think I am going to like this city.

September 1, 1986   My room

Back in my room to await AC's call, I take a nap. Phone rings at 2:30 pm—Ms Cao of computer fame (I met her with the delegation in New York last Christmas). She is meeting AC in his room at 4:00 pm.

I talk to AC. First he's heard of it. I repair to my room to work on telexes.

6:30 pm. Amid thunder and lightning we go to a restaurant called Chou En Mei or something for the banquet with the Minister of the P&T. Also present is the Deputy Minister of Science and Technology for the MPT and numerous others from last night. We are a party of eight, and roast duck is once again on the menu.

The power fails, and we eat by candlelight, a not uncommon occurrence, I understand. . . . The MPT wants to purchase Apollo workstations. They claim they have been around longer and are more reliable. This I must argue with their people in a day or so.

We break up around 8:30 pm and head back to the hotel. Beijing is alive and pretty, especially in the rain. . . . At the hotel AC's brother is there and we are later joined by his younger daughter, a pretty and pleasant young woman who speaks good English (for someone who has only been studying for six months! I am constantly amazed by the learning ability of the Chinese. I know Americans who have studied foreign languages for years and who cannot carry a conversation).

September 3, 1986   11:17 pm   Beijing Hotel

Pressure pumps fell through because they could not locate us in time; they signed with the Brits. Frequency changers look like ours. Nix on the hosiery machines: the president of Mastek is in Shijiazhuang now negotiating direct. Down to rubber hose and cold plate (both of which look weak from my point of view).

At about 2:30 pm, guests began arriving: soldering machine; mobile radio system; power cables. Then I went back and rested from 4:00 to 6:00 or so, then got up to have dinner with four engineers from the Railway Bureau.

We dined at the European-American Compound, which contains a restaurant right to the west of the hotel, across the street. I had seen the building during my walking tour.

Many toasts with a delicious sweet red wine made in China. More of a sherry than a wine. . . . Railroad people offered to take me to the Great Wall this Sunday. As it happens, though, I must instead go to Shijiazhuang (the capital of Hebei Province) on Sunday, to fight for the hose and hosiery business.

Back at the hotel, wrote (and sent) some telexes back to the States at about 10:30 pm (the telex office closes at 11:00 pm).

Tomorrow, an early start for the MicroVax II installation.

September 5, 1986   12:01 am   Beijing Hotel

Spent the day at the MVAX-2 location, supervising the dismantling of the crates. Ms. Wong was my interpreter, a charming young woman of thirty-three with a five-year-old daughter and a husband from Shanghai who has traveled to the US many times.

Ms. Cao was there (arrived during lunch with AC) and later on Dr. Li showed up, in mufti. The military barracks is so close you can hear the sergeant-major's whistle on the parade grounds. Was driven back to the hotel at 5:00 pm by Ms. Cao (who is going to Europe next month) and her driver . . . Rode alone in the back of the black car like a character in a Graham Greene novel, gliding through the rain-swept streets of Beijing, past Tian An Men Square . . .

Talked to Julia in New York after waiting nearly two hours for the connection.

Tomorrow: more MVAX-2, then 8200 presentation. Must sleep . . .

September 9, 1986   Hebei Guest House, Shijiazhuang   11:26 pm

Moment: In the Red Star Restaurant last night. Walking downstairs from the private dining rooms after dinner to the smoky, barnlike atmosphere of the public dining room. People half-rising from their seats. Pointing.

Moment: Today, the banquet for twenty-three people at the Beijing Duck Restaurant. Going upstairs to the private dining room. The same gawking, gesticulating, the whole noisy room turning silent as we appear like aliens from another planet. I to AC: "Floor show begins."

Moment: Last night, typing amendments and revisions to the frequency changer contract. Everyone coming to stare at the portable Sharp typewriter and marvel at the speed with which I type.

"Is it automatic?" someone asks.

"No," I reply in jest. "I must still type the words."

"Ah," they nod sagely, and continue to watch.

Moment: [a young computer technician from the MVAX-2 project] *telling me of the time Chinese troops returned from the Vietnam War (!) only to find China in the grip of the Proletarian Cultural Revolution. The Red Guard had established zones through which no one but the Red Guard could pass. A few soldiers crossed the chalk-marked line to chat with members of the Guard . . . and were shot dead.*

The other soldiers returned fire and killed four of the Red Guard. The Guard captured the soldiers and sentenced them to death, but Mao commuted their sentence.

Ms Wong had not heard of this story.

The young man well-informed about the United States. Talk briefly about Joe McCarthy.

September 11, 1986   Hebei Guest House, Shijiazhuang   12:34 am

At 12:15–12:20 am, in front of a TV crew and with the mayor of Shijiazhuang in attendance, we signed the rubber hose line contract.

The entire day had been a struggle over this contract, and for a moment we thought we had lost it for certain. Then, a phone call—and telex—from Julia (like a last moment cavalry charge) and the day was saved.

We beat RCM, a Swiss company that had made three trips here already and that has been battling for this contract for nearly a year. On September 3, they had signed a technical agreement with the factory (I signed one myself this afternoon) and they figured the contract was theirs, the signing a mere formality.

Today, the Swiss were informed of their loss. According to an eye-witness, they were understandably quite upset. They told the Chinese, "We have labored to build a bridge between our two organizations. You have broken this bridge. It will be very difficult for you to contact us again should you ever wish to." They were working through a Hong Kong agent, and the Swiss had been especially invited by the provincial government to participate in the project. There were no competitors until we arrived and, in seventy-two hours, "snatched the meat from the tiger's mouth" in the words of AC.

I must ask myself sometimes what is going on. Two years ago I would not have visualized myself in China making million dollar deals happen, but here I am. I could visualize myself in China, alright, but not as a salesman or technical consultant on engineering matters, but as a tourist seeking after those places spoken of in Taoist legend: the temples hidden on mountaintops in the midst of impossible scenery, or secreted in caves or in the squares of small villages; or at Buddhist shrines, drinking in the tangkas and the smell of old incense, the sight of ancient monks keeping the faith alive by blowing on its embers.

I could have seen myself retracing the steps of the Long March, maybe, or wandering the *hutongs* in search of some trembling memory within myself of a China that was, and of some love I must have felt there, for while the memory is sad it is also somehow warm.

But standing once again, in front of TV crews . . . shaking the mayor's hand, smiling, waving in the elevator, at the lights and the applause . . . no, never.

AC understandably happy. Elated. Shook hands. Congratulated each other. Laughed.

We beat the Japanese in Shenzhen, the Germans in Baoding, and now the Swiss—the poor, neutral Swiss—in Shijiazhuang. And we never actually see them, the competition, but we know they're there. The negotiations—which are tough, demanding, exhausting, frustrating—tell us they're there. And how, why, do we beat them? We are from the USA. USA is "in" now in the PRC, and everybody wants to go there.

A man was part of the negotiation in an observer role the last two days or so. His name is Guo, and he is with the Hebei Petrochemical Organization. His father studied at the University of Texas, at Austin, and returned to China after the Revolution, where he was considered to be a spy (as were all returning Chinese at that time) and sent to forced labor. His son, Mr. Guo, learned to speak very good English via the tape recorder and a TV program called *Follow Me* (put out by the Brits). Presumably, he also listens to the Voice of America, like everyone else I meet who speaks English.

We leave tomorrow on the 2:00 pm train for Beijing. More work awaits us, of course. We must sign the formal wire machinery contract, or what happened to the Swiss could easily happen to us. I have my MicroVAX-2 people waiting for me (another week of that at least) and yet more projects. I should have brought winter clothing . . .

Before that first trip was over, we were quoting a total of twenty-six different projects at once. In those days, China was the Wild West. There were projects flying everywhere. It was almost impossible to keep up with the constant demands for quotations, proposals, technical specifications, contract rewrites, requotes, and more requotes. I did not get back to the States until the middle of November, and then I was back in Beijing in December to sign a few more contracts over the Christmas holidays.

But the people . . . the minister and the vice-ministers were men of worldly sophistication and grace; the Communist Party officials at the various factories were uniformly dour, humorless, and suspicious; the engineers and technical specialists in the rural area factories were rude, insulting, and more than once accused me of lying or of being stupid and incompetent; contract specialists would attempt to correct my English, claiming they spoke it better; and then there were the quiet, pleasant, older men and women who had been through hell during the Cultural Revolution.

You could always tell who they were. They had the bent backs, nervous tics, swollen, misshapen fingers and red-chapped hands that were evidence of a decade of hard labor and physical torture in the re-education camps. Like the Jimmy Stewart character in the movie *Harvey*, they found that it was better to be nice than to be clever, and they smiled that faint half-smile of former prisoners of war now sitting in a room surrounded by the very people who had left them to rot in the camps. They had loved Mao in the beginning, in those heady days before the Great Leap Forward, just after the Revolution and the proclamation of the People's Republic of China in Tian An Men Square in 1949, when no one locked their doors and everyone shared everything in common. Then, Mao's face had turned against them and by the time of the Great Proletarian Cultural Revolution, which began in 1966, they were the enemies of the people; their Father had rejected them.

There is a saying in China that "The Party is like the Sun, and the Leader of the Party is like the Moon: sometimes bright, sometimes dark." That's one way of describing it, I guess.

But they are the decision-makers in China, this generation that came of age during and after the Revolution; and those that were born in the dawn of New China and lived just long enough to suffer the ravages of the Cultural Revolution. Mao, to these individuals, is like an Old Testament God: the Creator of the State, and the source of all Wrath. No single Chinese has had such an effect on the psyches of the country since the time of Confucius. For that reason, it is useless to speak of Lao Tzu and the *Dao De Jing* when trying to understand China and the Chinese business people you will meet and with whom you will negotiate one day; Mao ridiculed the way of the Dao, claiming it represented antisocial and antirevolutionary greedy self-interest. He might have been right, if the China of today is any indication. But the "China of today" is his legacy to the world, not Lao Tzu's.

> **Idealism and metaphysics are the easiest things in the world, because people can talk as much nonsense as they like without basing it on a objective reality or having it tested against that reality.**
>
> **—Chairman Mao**

The China of the Dao, of Confucius, of martial arts and calligraphy, of Buddhism and the *I Jing* is the China of popular culture and the China of the academician. It, too, is a virtual reality: something created in a library or a classroom, or in Hollywood or sentimental novels. It's the China we, in the West, *prefer* to think about. You'll find traces of it there, especially now that the Chinese have discovered the China of our invention and find it useful for attracting tourists and investors. The Chinese government has relaxed its policy on religion, re-opening famous temples because they realized that overseas Chinese would flock to them, to worship in the old places reverenced by their grandparents and their grandparents' grandparents. Some of these temples are staffed by cadres, loyal Communists who dress like novice monks and keep an eye on the till.

We want to believe in China, we foreigners and Westerners. We want to believe that there are no grudges, no suspicions, no paranoid fantasies brewing behind those pleasant faces that we see in the travel posters and the television documentaries. We want to believe that we are all friends, now. We want to believe in the Dao.

But before we can get to the Dao, we have to get through the Mao.

> **We should help the masses to realize that we represent their interests, that our lives are intimately bound up with theirs.**
>
> **—Chairman Mao**

This is useful advice, not just for approaching your customers in China but in handling your people back home. China can become such an all-consuming proposition that you will appear to have lost perspective, or are willing to sacrifice your company's assets in the pursuit of the "white whale" of China trade. One also should pay particular attention to the second part of the above quotation: you must make both your customers and your own company realize that your life is intimately bound up with theirs . . . and vice versa. They must identify as strongly as possible with your stated goals.

In China, this is done through the methods we have already described: the banquets, the drinking, the karaoke. By exposing your life to theirs, and by developing your customers as friends, you have identified your life with theirs to a large extent. That is why rotating personnel into and out of China is such a mistake: it dilutes the very strength that your company has created there, the personal bond between the decision-makers on both sides.

Back home, by creating a "revolutionary spirit" among your own cadres you can be assured of their support for your endeavors. Do not for one moment believe that because your employees work for you and earn a salary that they will do all they can to ensure your success overseas. The additional work and additional "head space" that China requires will become a burden and will be resisted as much as possible. Even slight resistance—a slight inattention to detail, for example—can sink your China junk before it hits open water. You need your people behind you, from the CEO to the shipping department and mail room; everyone has to be on board.

Production by the masses, the interests of the masses, the experiences and feelings of the masses—to these the leading cadres should pay constant attention.

—Chairman Mao

There are people in our leading organs in some places who think that it is enough for the leaders alone to know the Party's policies and that there is no need to let the masses know them. This is one of the basic reasons why some of our work cannot be done well.

—Chairman Mao

You can put this philosophy to work in several ways, and I recommend using all of them.

When I was abroad, I made sure that the people back home got a kind of newsletter from me from time to time, informing them of my progress and spicing it up with some anecdotes from my trip. In the old days, this was done via telex and the only person I had to entertain was Julia (mentioned in my notes above). Later, it was done by fax and now it's by email. I make sure that everyone gets a copy, which includes them in the effort and makes them feel like part of the campaign (which they are, of course, but everyone likes to be reminded of that fact once in awhile).

Second, when I was back home I managed to visit all the departments personally the first day or so that I was back in the office. This way, my efforts became personalized and they could identify me with the newsletters. Everyone always had questions or comments, and by interacting with them I made them part of the actual team. I could listen to their reactions, understand the problems they faced in dealing with their own aspect of China trade, and come up with solutions, nipping problems in the bud before they became unmanageable.

Last, on one or two occasions, I was able to make a speech on the factory floor. We would gather the workers together—a break in the day is always appreciated, regardless of the reason!—and I would tell them, briefly, what was going on and how their work impacted not only the company's bottom line but how they were helping to defeat our competitors in China. Factory workers are as cynical in the States as they are in China, and I was under no illusion that my remarks would be greeted with a rousing "Huzzah!" . . . but I knew that what I said would simmer in their minds long after I was gone on another trip to the mysterious East and that they would take a little more pride in what they were doing, a little more care in processing the orders, a little more attention to the intricacies of the paperwork.

Then there is your China staff.

> **Ask your subordinates about matters you don't understand or don't know, and do not lightly express your approval or disapproval. . . . We should never pretend to know what we don't know, we should "not feel ashamed to ask and learn from people below" and we should listen carefully to the views of the cadres at the lower levels. Be a pupil before you become a teacher . . .**
> **—Chairman Mao**

We can learn a lot from the above quotation. In my experience, companies that do not behave this way often fail miserably, and especially when it comes to foreign trade. In China, your local staff is your teacher, your guru, your entrée into a world you can never hope to know completely. They may not know very much about your company or its product line at first, but do not mistake that kind of ignorance with general ignorance. The people you will work with in China are among the brightest and most motivated in the world. They will work long and hard to make your mission a success because they want to be proud of their involvement with you, and of their own accomplishments. If you ignore their advice, however, or do not extend yourself a little to understand their backgrounds, their capabilities, and their perspectives on what you are doing, you could be asking for trouble.

One of the problems of Western executives in China is basically that of attitude. Part of that stems from the stress they are under to perform well and to meet their financial obligations to the bottom line. That's hard enough to do at home, but when you're ten thousand miles away in a foreign country, the stakes have just become higher. That attitude gets communicated to their local staff, and misunderstandings arise.

One can take a patronizing attitude to the local people working for you, communicating one's lack of respect or lack of confidence in the staff. Without putting it into words, the communication still takes place. By keeping staff members away from the decision-making process, you essentially devalue their role and keep them in a subordinate position. While this happens often enough in the United States, when you are in China you face a different set of challenges. Your staff is local, you are not: you're a foreigner, an outsider, in some cases you are still referred to as a "devil" or a "white ghost" even though no one takes those terms seriously anymore. They feel, and rightly, that they understand their country and its market better than you do. Your edge over them is actually quite limited: your company, your product.

Your attitude may say to them: you need me more than I need you. That is not true, of course. Without them you don't have a chance in their country.

The other approach taken by some executives, especially the inexperienced ones, is to go in the other direction and give too much power and authority to the staff. This means that you have ceded your responsibility for the outcome of the mission to people whose first loyalties are to their families, their neighborhoods, and their country (pretty much in that order). Generally speaking, Chinese people do not understand how one can be loyal to a corporation. A corporation is not a person, not a member of the family. In old China, families ran companies, so obviously everyone was loyal within the company since they were all related. With the coming of the industrial age—which came rather late to China—the factory replaced the company; but since Mao had initiated the "iron rice bowl" situation in which every worker was guaranteed a job for life, no one could be fired so no one felt any need for loyalty.

Now, with privatization and the explosive growth of new companies whose only rationale is profit in the capitalist sense, Chinese entrepreneurs have been unleashed on the market. For the first time since the Revolution, companies were closing and people were losing their jobs due to the unprofitability of the old paradigm. Once again, there was no reason for corporate loyalty. There has been little or no precedent for the type of corporate identification that we have (or used to have) in the West: no gold watch after twenty or thirty years of service. In case you hadn't noticed, corporate loyalty is also disappearing in the West due to down-sizing and outsourcing. If you cannot trust your company to be loyal to you as an employee, then obviously there can be no loyalty in the other direction.

This type of attitude seems cynical or somehow dishonest or unethical to the Western executive, but this is because the Chinese are not so hypocritical about it. Your employees will leave your office if they find a slightly better job at a slightly bigger firm for slightly more money. The amount of jumping between jobs is crazy in China, especially within the same industry. Holding on to good people will be a challenge, and the best way to deal with that challenge is to take Mao's advice and include them as much as possible in what you are doing and thinking. Ask for their suggestions, keep them involved, and show them respect. Learn from them, they have a lot to teach.

Employing Chinese workers is a another thorny issue from a legal standpoint in China. Your workers will come to you from a government agency and their salaries will be paid into that agency. You can, however, manage to create a kind of profit-sharing situation in which they receive bonuses at various times throughout the year, particularly at the time of Chinese New Year. There are other ways to reward your staff as well, such as trips to other cities or even in some cases trips abroad if they can be arranged. These are ways of keeping and motivating local staff.

> Place problems on the table. . . . Do not talk behind people's backs. Whenever problems arise, call a meeting, place the problems on the table for discussion, take some decisions and the problems will be solved.
>
> —Chairman Mao

Jealousy will be an issue, however. Promoting someone before another will always give rise to bad feelings. Seniority counts for a lot, and if you give one employee any special attention or benefits before they are scheduled for them you are guaranteed to have problems with the other members of your staff.

Although flattery is as useful in China as elsewhere, it can give the employee the mistaken impression that they can do no wrong. Others will resent him or her, and internecine intrigues will ensue. Remember that China is only now coming out of a "collectivist" mentality and into a more "individualist" phase. Before, one was expected to criticize oneself in front of a crowd of fellow workers and colleagues and Party officials; if you were intelligent, or accomplished, or educated, you might wind up in the labor camps. China at the time of the Cultural Revolution was very much a country of the "lowest common denominator," a country where conformity was valued more than individual accomplishment or ability. In fact, individual capabilities were a liability, because it implied that you knew you were somehow better—not only different, but better—than your fellow citizens, and this was anathema to the Revolution. This has changed now, but people are still a little uncomfortable with the transition. This is true of people in their forties and fifties now; the younger university students are not so old-fashioned in their thinking and have embraced a more aggressive attitude toward life and achieving their goals, but it also means that if you are not living up to their expectations of what a Western company and a Western business executive should be and do, then they will leave for greener pastures.

One problem you will face is that quite often your staff members will not tell you what is bothering them face-to-face. You are still a foreigner, and some of what they dislike or resent will be impossible to tell you up front. That is why you should rely on the services of your original sales agent as much as possible when it comes to staff issues.

If you are still employing the agent, you can have him interview your staff members before they are hired so you can get his or her impression of their character, personality, and suitability. I have found it useful to place the agent on the staff, as the office manager or the general manager of the office, if the agent has administrative experience and can deal with people well in that capacity. Otherwise, you will be the manager and will have to develop a methodology for interacting with your employees to maximize their contribution and solve any problems that may arise.

One way of doing this is to treat them the way you would a customer, which, in a sense, is what they are. Bonding with the employees can be very rewarding and can get them to open up to you. Sometimes only a chance word will be all they are willing to reveal, but it will usually be enough. Taking the staff out to dinner is always a good idea; be careful of taking individual members, though, because that will only lead to jealousy and gossip. It's better to take them all out at once so you can demonstrate your impartiality. The reason why your customers want to get to know you in different social situations is precisely the reason why you should submit your staff members to the same test: the social situation of a dinner, perhaps followed by some good-natured karaoke singing, will reveal to you the strengths and stresses that are at play among your staff. Who smiles, who does not; who sings, who does not; who drinks, and how much, and how it affects them; these are all ways of not only understanding your individual staff members but also of revealing their inter-relationships, which will tell you something about what is going on under the radar.

No one should be praised above another; no one should receive any benefits that the others do not. All should be treated equally, or as equally as possible. Problems should be identified and addressed quickly, before they get out of hand. China is the Kingdom of Gossip, and sometimes it can be quite deadly. It is better to reduce the amount of gossip by reducing the number of opportunities for it to flourish.

And, finally, one way I found to reduce the amount of employee dissatisfaction and sabotage was to go back to an ancient Chinese tradition: at my last office in Beijing, I hired staff members who were all related to each other! While that seems like a kind of nepotism in Western eyes, it worked quite well for the office. There was no gossip, no jealousy, and everyone worked together for the common goal.

Chapter 9
The Overall China Strategy, Summarized

Reading is learning, but applying is also learning and the more important kind of learning at that.
—Chairman Mao

Chairman Mao has had a lot to tell us about his country, his people, and the way to conduct a guerrilla campaign. Just the way that Sun Tzu's *Art of War* is being used to re-imagine business strategy, Mao's *Quotations* can be used to better understand the Chinese business environment today. The face of the Chairman still looms, huge and grinning, over the entrance to the Forbidden City. The further you go into the countryside, the more Mao jackets you will see. Mao Ze Dong has made his indelible mark on his country and on the psyches of his people. Together with Chiang Kai Shek he defeated the Japanese invaders; then he turned on Chiang and sent him packing to Taiwan. American forces assisted Chiang in his fight against the Japanese and, half-heartedly, in his struggle with Mao. Eventually, the Americans realized that Chiang was little more than a mobster and abandoned him to his fate.

The Chinese still hold Taiwan against us. We supported the government of Taiwan for decades after the end of the Second World War and the Revolution of 1949. We didn't recognize China—and "de-recognize" Taiwan—until the 1970s. But the two countries are still in an official state of war. If you buy a map of China in any bookstore from Beijing to Urumqi, it will always include the island nation of Taiwan as just another province. If you buy a map of "China" in Taipei, you see the same thing: not just the island the Portuguese, called Formosa, but the whole Asian landmass we call the Peoples Republic of China, renamed the Republic of China.

China as virtual reality.

Then there is the China of the business books that focus on the ancient sages like Sun Tzu and Lao Tzu, and the China of the recent histories, which are just now struggling to interpret the country in terms of Mao and his legacy while straining to retain the academician's proper distance from the subject matter.

China as virtual reality.

There is the China of Mao chic: the fashion trend among the young that idealizes the Grand Old Man and ignores his hideous excesses. The *Little Red Book* has become fodder for song lyrics, and pictures of Mao adorn fancy new restaurants. It's the China of bars, sex, rock, and the occasional designer drug.

More virtual reality.

What, then, is the real China?

It's the China of the seven hundred million people who never made it to the karaoke bars, the shopping malls, or a decent meal. They're the people Mao referred to as "the masses," the backbone of his revolution. They're the ones who have been there since before recorded history, working the same fields, bearing children, suffering under one regime or the next. They're the ones who will become your customers in the next ten or twenty years, as more and more of them either wind up in the cities, looking for work and for homes, for small luxuries and a better life; or selling their farms for more money than they ever dreamed of having and looking to buy the larger luxuries of life. Keep your eye on this exploding population, this new wave of internal immigration that is moving from the remote provinces and farms to places like Beijing and Shanghai and Guangzhou, Chengdu and Chongqing, Nanjing and Hangzhou. The effect they will have and are beginning to have on the markets you are looking at now will be profound. New demand for utilities, housing, schools, construction of all kinds, communication and transportation services, medical services, and additional policing will provide new opportunities for the entrepreneur and investor. The major Chinese cities are in the process of total transformation. The Beijing and Shanghai of today look nothing like those same cities of only twenty years ago, and they are getting ready to change again. Anyone who tells you that the market is "mature" and that you are too late, that your competitors have it sewn up, that there's no room for another player is not living in the real China, but in their own private China: China as virtual reality.

I would like to re-emphasize some of the points already made for the sake of underlining their importance. Your first step is making your initial contacts in China. You may have already been approached by an agent or a company. By now, you know how to handle that contact. You should offer no money up front, you should ask for some details of previous business, references, that sort of thing. You should freely offer sales information (nonproprietary) technical information, whatever else the agent or company asks for, short of an actual quote until you have a good idea what's going on. And feel free to ask the agent for any information you feel you need before making a commitment to your first trip, your first venture into the market. You have probably been doing a lot of reading—books, magazine articles—about China trade and the Chinese business environment. Do not be shy when it comes to asking your agent for clarification or to expand on some of the themes you have been reading. Of course, just because he or she is a specialist in getting jobs and making a percentage does not automatically make them a PhD in

China studies, so don't be surprised if they can't answer some specific questions that you have gleaned from reading Western perspectives on China.

When it comes to others in your field or industry who have been to China, listen to what they have to say and pick up any pointers or anecdotes that might be useful but don't make the mistake of believing that they are "Old China Hands" just because they've been there a few times. Their China is also virtual reality. It's a little like freshmen looking up to seniors: the seniors still haven't graduated or made their way in the real world, so don't be too intimidated or impressed. Your experiences will be different; draw your own conclusions about what you see and hear. Your China is as valid as anyone else's.

You may be appalled at what appears to be a general lack of hygiene. People routinely spit in the streets; young children wear special pants that allow them to squat wherever they happen to be for a bowel movement; sometimes when dining, you will note that some people spit out their bones onto the floor or, in a really nice place, directly onto the table in front of them. However, they view our habits as equally disgusting: I mean, who would actually pick a bone out of their mouth with their fingers and then roll it up in a napkin as it were some kind of gift for the waiter? Gross.

Eating a meal with chopsticks in China, some observers have felt that the Chinese are unconcerned with hygiene because they use their sticks on the dishes in front of them: in other words, they are eating with the same sticks that they stick into the food that you are about to eat. Gross.

Except that the people who make these observations do not understand that the Chinese are far more expert at using the sticks than they are. A Chinese diner does not rummage around in the dish in front of her, but selects the piece she will take in advance and then narrows in for the kill, touching only the piece that has been selected. A Chinese diner will never use their own sticks to pick out a piece for you (although it is quite common for your host to show his or her respect by choosing a particularly choice morsel and putting it on your plate . . . using a pair of chopsticks especially provided for the purpose). It's the Chinese diners who are a little nervous of foreigners at the table, what with sloppy chopstick technique and picking bones out of their mouths and wrapping them in napkins . . .

What does this gloss have to do with your business strategy? It's just another attempt to show you that your conclusions about what you see can be quite wrong. If we disagree on such basic concepts as hygiene and dining, then how many more things do we not understand about each other? Open your mind when you go to China; take your time to absorb and digest the country. This is your new market, after all. It could be your biggest market. It will certainly be the one that will make the most impression on your company, and on your company's bottom line. Don't treat it as you would a small town in your home country. China is not a country of bumpkins and simpletons; they are some of the smartest people in the world, whose only obstacles at the moment are grinding poverty and a government that is not sure how to manage the capitalist economy. These things will be solved, some gradually, some sooner than you think. Don't blind yourself to the opportunities by generalizing or trivializing what you see and hear.

Do not attempt to go after the whole market at once. Be careful of spreading yourself and your company too thin. The temptation will be great: there is always another project, even bigger, over the horizon: in the next town, the next province, the next city. Restrain yourself and think through every new development carefully and soberly.

Do not rely on your customer's interpreter. When possible, take along your own. The customer's interpreter may be great at translating English and Mandarin, but there is no guarantee that someone else's interpreter will have your best interests at heart. Your interpreter will be able to gauge the reactions of your customers in ways that the customer's interpreter will never dream of doing.

Your interpreter will give you an idea of what is not being interpreted by the other side. Your interpreter is your eyes and ears on the other side of the negotiating table, so make sure that you are in synch. Develop a signal system if you have to, some means of communicating during a conference that no one else will notice. This way, the other side's interpreter will not be able to figure out what your interpreter is telling you if there is something delicate or interesting taking place.

Do not shout or scream or stamp your foot or pound your fist. No matter how frustrated or aggravated you become, never let them see you sweat. When you lose your emotional composure, you have revealed your weakness and your strategy to the other side. You never want to do that in China (or anywhere else, for that matter). Never expose your deepest thoughts by reacting emotionally to what happens in front of you. During the Korean War, the West used to think that the Chinese were masters of interrogation and brainwashing. Actually, our term "brainwashing" is a translation of the Chinese phrase. By sitting there peacefully in front of you, smiling and telling you the most outrageous lie or asking you for the impossible, they are not being serious: they are testing you, trying to find out just how flexible you are and how willing to negotiate. If you react negatively, they will—smilingly and politely—show you the door. Never say "no." Always leave room for further negotiation.

And when you have finally signed a project or two, it's time to seriously consider opening some kind of office in China (and I don't mean in Hong Kong, as attractive as that may seem). You can use your agent for this, give him a title and install him in some small space somewhere in Beijing or Shanghai. Even if your business is outside these cities, some of your customers want an excuse to visit and if you have an office there they will cheerfully endure the ten hours on an overcrowded train to meet you for tea and karaoke. Of course, if your business is heavily concentrated in Szechuan Province, for example, then it will behoove you to have an office in Chengdu or Chongqing or somewhere close to where the action is. It raises the comfort level of your customers and makes getting future business a lot easier.

As mentioned previously, use local resources for advertising and marketing as much as possible. It's cheaper and better designed. You do not want to be shipping brochures back and forth across the seas because of mistakes in translation or some other problem. Send the art and the copy to China and let them take it from there.

As frequently as possible, set up seminars and lunches in as many provinces as you can, especially in the first few years of your campaign. The customers need to see you, touch and feel your product, and sit through your technical and sales presentations. Always give little gifts to your attendees, not only corporate brochures. Getting pens made with your corporate logo, or pen knives, wallets, little leather notebooks, that sort of thing is also inexpensive in China and are the sorts of things they will never throw away. Always throw in lunch.

Be prepared for every eventuality. You may lose power during a presentation or something else may go wrong. Have a back-up plan. Allow enough days between presentations in different cities to provide for transportation snafus.

Invest in those little handy packets of facial tissue and carry at least one or two with you at all times. The availability of toilet tissue in some areas is rather metaphysical.

The Chinese smoke, and they smoke like the proverbial chimneys. You will get nowhere by complaining about it. If you are a recovering smoker, then you have my sympathy. I have never smoked tobacco in my life, but there is every possibility that I have inhaled more smoke than a reporter at a presidential press conference.

If you are a recovering alcoholic, once again my sympathy. The Chinese drink; they don't have HBO so what else are they going to do? (Well . . . of course . . . *that*, but there is a one family, one child policy in China.) If you do not wish to drink, my advice is to claim some kind of medical reason, hypertension or an allergy or an ulcer.

This will allow both of you to save face, and you will not be expected to drink.

Sex. The Chinese are not prudish about sex, and it is a dirty little nonsecret that Chinese men have mistresses, second wives, affairs, dalliances with prostitutes, and so forth. When you are with Chinese men during a business negotiation and everyone decides to call it a night and have dinner and drinks, the subject of women will inevitably come up. As their guest, they may invite you to a karaoke club where there is ready availability of women. Or you may feel you have to invite them. This is another test.

Some American executives that I know have openly balked at this, and have refused to have anything to do with it. One's moral and ethical and religious beliefs are one's own, so far be it from me to disparage them. However, you are not a missionary out to proselytize the Chinese so there is no use in displaying your disgust, umbrage, outrage, or . . . fear . . . at this development. As the Chinese always say, "We're not expecting you to *marry* the woman." *Exactly*, your conscience tells you. *This is sex outside of marriage!* So, what to do?

You could always claim a medical reason, but it would probably not be believed and, anyway, the Chinese may be a little leery of dealing with someone with a social disease. The best thing is to brass it out. No one is going to be watching you *in flagrante* (well, hopefully not the Public Security Bureau), so the ideal strategy is to appear to have taken the young lady to your room for the usual reasons and then politely decline her services when you are alone. She may expect a tip anyway, and it is probably best to pay it just so that everyone involved "saves face."

Corruption. As I mentioned earlier on, you must not become involved in bribery under any circumstances. You could be arrested, either by the Chinese or by your own country, depending on its laws. Bribery is something that is best handled off-camera and off-stage. You don't need to know about it.

I know I will be criticized for confronting this most essential issue of doing business in China (and in many other countries) in this manner, but let's all be realistic here. It's going to happen. It may even be happening with your money, and you won't know it. Keep it that way. If your sales agent knows his or her business, then if it has to be handled it will be handled. Somehow. It has nothing to do with you. It will not appear on your books. There will be no photographs of you handing over an envelope full of cash (it doesn't work that way, anyway).

If you hold serious religious or ethical concerns about this, though, then China trade is probably not for you. Think of it this way: you pay your agent a commission, right? If your agent then pays someone else a commission, where is the crime or the wrongdoing? I am not trying to convince you to go down the rocky road of corrupt practices; just the opposite, in fact. Avoid it like the plague, but in the immortal words of a previous Fearless Leader, "Don't ask, don't tell."

Getting paid. My advice is to stick with the letter of credit system and completely avoid credit issues and 30-60-90-day payment terms. It is almost impossible to chase debtors in China with any degree of satisfaction. Get the cash upfront in the form of a Letter of Credit drawn on a US bank, usually through Bank of China, which is the state-run bank most often used for these transactions. If you must extend credit, then please invest in export insurance. You'll thank me for this advice.

Shipping the goods. Very carefully. Pack well, double pack, and make sure that there is no way water, sand, heat, cold, or anything else could damage your products. You're not shipping a few hundred miles downstream; you're shipping over vast distances in all kinds of transport to a factory somewhere in China's heartland. Imagine that you were that shipment. How secure would you want to be packed?

Documentation. Companies have fallen over this very issue. Make absolutely certain that your documentation—shipping documents, invoices, packing lists, etc.—are in pristine and accurate condition. Have someone trustworthy on your staff back home take charge of this aspect of your business. Faulty documentation means you won't get paid. It's that simple, and that dire.

Travel to China. You still need a visa to get into China, so my recommendation is to fly into Hong Kong first (always a popular option!) and get your Chinese visa through any hotel travel agency, preferably the one where you are staying the night. You will have the visa the next day. If you are planning on multiple trips (and who isn't?) then make sure you get a multiple entry visa, which will save you a lot of time and money in the future. They are usually good for six months for any number of trips.

Which takes me to my next point: do not plan on a couple of days in China then a return home. It would be pointless. Take your time each trip. Spend at least two weeks if you can, more if possible. You need face time with your agent, your customers, and your staff (if any). You need to be around and to show that you care about the market and will be around tomorrow.

Plan several trips a year, at the bare minimum. Don't worry, those frequent flyer miles will add up and soon you will be upgrading to business class. If you show up in China every quarter, then people will begin to trust you and to rely upon you. It will also give you an opportunity to see China in every kind of weather, which is also beneficial in the long run as you quote machinery or electronics that can be affected by drastic weather changes.

Learn to eat Chinese. Don't spend every spare moment in the Western-style café or restaurant in your hotel. Get acclimated to your new surroundings, and insist to your agent that you spend time among "the masses." Getting to know your environment is essential to the success of your guerrilla campaign. That kind of knowledge will pay dividends further down the road you go.

Do not give up on China if you experience a failure or setback. It's not the end of the world. You will lose some projects to your competitors. It's inevitable, and it's no criticism of your strategy or of your customer base. You never know what is going on behind the scenes in every negotiation. Always remain positive and upbeat, especially in front of your customers and staff. There will *always* be more work in China. Always.

Mao suffered several setbacks in the course of the Revolution. One of these was known as the Long March, when he was forced to retreat a great distance. But Mao didn't call retreat a form of failure; he referred to it as a defensive strategy. That sounds like "spin" but he was right, after all. He eventually won, and the Long March became a symbol of the Revolution's resiliency and staying power and not as a symbol of defeat or failure. There may be times when you have to retreat; when you do, make sure it's part of an overall strategy for success.

Mao, of course, would be horrified to learn that I am using his words, his thought, and his theories as inspiration for a new capitalist methodology. But how do you think Lao Tzu feels? That eminent Chinese sage who believed in going with the flow, who abandoned society and the emperor in order to go back to the wilderness and disappear quietly into Nature . . . would be mad as hell that his words and ideas have inspired several writers in their books on China trade. Imagine Henry David Thoreau's work being used by a petroleum company or quotations from *Walden* as bumper stickers on the back of a Hummer.

But truth is truth. Wisdom is wisdom. Mao was wise, pragmatic, focused. He was not just the Chairman . . . he was the Chairman of the Board. As many mistakes as he made during his later years—and there were a lot of them—it was his foresight and dedication that liberated China from centuries of feudalism and oppression. China has suffered greatly in the last century, but the Chinese now stand proud of their country and its accomplishments and are excited about where the country is heading in the next hundred years.

Napoleon Bonaparte once wrote: When China awakes, the world will tremble.

Do you feel a tremor?

Appendix
A Short Primer on Survival Mandarin

You won't be able to speak Mandarin by reading this appendix, but with any luck you will be able to recognize key words and phrases after you have been in China for a while and get used to the pronunciation.

The type of Mandarin spoken in Beijing has a rather harsh sound when compared to the Mandarin spoken in Taiwan, for instance. Some observers have referred to Beijing Mandarin as the cackle of a Beijing Duck. When I first went to China, the Mandarin I studied in New York had a specific accent that was unmistakable, like American Gothic Chinese, or something. After a few months of working with Anthony Chang, people remarked that my accent sounded like I came from Shandong Province (which is where AC came from). A few years after that, and my accent shifted to that of a Beijing taxi driver. I much prefer the latter.

One of the biggest problems for foreigners learning Mandarin is the tonal nature of the language. Westerners are used to speech that relies upon the correct pronunciation of consonants and vowels in their proper order; Chinese, however, rely more on how the individual syllable is pronounced as a whole: the tone of the syllable. There are four such tones in Mandarin, so consider yourself lucky. There are nine in Cantonese, and that isn't even the worst. Nine different ways to say the same vowel-consonant combination. Yikes.

For the sake of information, the four tones are:
Rising
Falling
Falling-rising
High
There is also a fifth "non tone."

You won't be able to mimic these tones by reading a book, so don't even try. The best you can hope for right now is to memorize some of the following words and phrases so that you might be able to pick them out of a discussion taking place around you. Do not assume, however, that you are right when you believe you have heard one of these phrases. Keep that suspicion to yourself and wait for the interpretation. You might have been dangerously wrong. At the same time, pay close attention anyway and see if you can identify key phrases. If you can, then you are well on your way to learning enough Mandarin to survive a business trip.

For the sake of consistency, I will use the common Romanization of the Chinese characters known as "pinyin" in China. You already know that Chinese languages are written in a kind of hieroglyphic, a "character" that is often made up of one or more root characters. These characters are said to have phonetic components. Ha! Don't believe it for a second. They are also said to have clues as to their meaning hidden in the arrangement of the strokes and in the root characters that make up the composite character. Ha! again. If you try to learn Mandarin that way, you are doomed to failure. Take it from me.

How Far Is It from Peking to Beijing?

Many of you are of an age when the capitol city of China was written "Peking." Then, a few decades ago, people started spelling it "Beijing." Was there a name change? Did they move the capitol? Those wily Chinese, what will they think of next?

Actually, it's the same place and it's pronounced exactly the same way.

Then, what happened?

It's like this. Some smarter-than-was-good-for-us missionaries decided they would try to create a Romanization of Mandarin, which would enable them to communicate more easily with those in the West. In order to create this new form of written Mandarin, they had to come up with some rules. One of these was that the letter "P" would represent the sound of "B," unless it was accompanied by an apostrophe in which case it would just be the same old letter "P" we know and love. Further, they decided that the letter "K" would represent the sound of "J". . . unless it was accompanied by an apostrophe, in which case it would remain the letter "K." Is that clear?

In other words, "Peking" was always meant to be pronounced "Beijing." Had it been written "P'e k'ing" it would have been pronounced "Peking." Sadly, no one thought to inform the rest of us of these arcane and somewhat illogical rules, with the result that generations of Westerners have been saying Peking instead of Beijing because that's how the word looks in print.

The *I Ching* is really the *I Jing*. You guessed it: if "Ch" was by itself, it would be pronounced as "J" . . . if it had an apostrophe, it would remain "Ch." And so forth. If you look around you will see I Jing spelled as I Ching, Yee Ching, Yee King, etc. because no one could quite agree on the Romanizations to be used. Hence the *pinyin* ("spell sound") system of the Chinese government which was invented to settle that problem once and for all. It is by far the easiest and most sensible of the methods employed, but there are a few letters which represent sounds that don't quite exist in English or other Western languages and that sometimes causes confusion in those who read it as if they are reading letters in their own tongue.

What I have done here is to reproduce the *pinyin* form exactly, and then give my own attempt at a pronunciation that would make sense to an English speaker. It is by no means precise—it couldn't be—but it gives you the vowel and consonant sounds approximating the actual. As I mentioned above, I won't even try to note the tones for each word, as that would only serve to confuse you and needlessly clutter up the text. The tones are important, of course, but my purpose here is not to help you speak Mandarin but to help you listen for it. Some syllable combinations—such as *he tong* for "contract"—you will pick up right away. Also, I have not grouped the syllables together into words, i.e., I write *he tong* instead of the more common *hetong*. The reason for this is to enable you to recognize some word groups that use the same syllables, such as *shi jia* (market price) and *dan jia* (unit price), thus revealing that the word *jia* means price and therefore *shi* is market and *dan* is unit.

Naturally, not all times the word *shi* appears does it mean "market." It can also mean "ten" or "is" or dozens of other words depending on context, on tone, and on the other syllable with which it is connected. This is not a Chinese dictionary or grammar, just a gentle guide into the shark-infested waters of Mandarin.

I also refrain from giving the Chinese characters for the words listed here. The reason is simple: it won't help you right now. Later, I recommend you picking up a good Chinese dictionary (they will almost all be Mandarin dictionaries; try finding a dictionary of Shanghainese or Hokkien . . .) and getting familiar with some of the characters for the words shown below. This way you will be able to recognize a contract when it comes in the mail and not confuse it with an ad for shaving cream. There are also a lot of good conversational Mandarin books available, some of which you can pick up at the airports in China. They will usually have the Chinese characters for the words and phrases they offer, so when all else fails you can point.

When to Say "No"

Never, actually. There is no word for "no" in Mandarin. There is no word for "yes." There are negatives, of course, but they change according to the verb they are negating. For instance, *mei you* (pronounced "may yo") means "don't have." It's a phrase you will hear constantly in China. "Do you have any Diet Coke?" "*Mei you.*" "Do you have the contract?" "*Mei you.*" "Is there space on the nine o'clock flight out of here?" "*Mei you.*" The word *you* means "have." The word *mei* does not mean "no," it is a negative that is used with the word *you*.

Conversely, the phrase *bu yao* (pronounced "boo yow") means "don't want." "Some sautéed scorpion for our foreign friend?" "*Bu yao!*" The word *yao* means "want," and the word *bu* is the negative you use with the word *yao*. You can't say *bu you*, just like you can't say *mei yao*.

If someone asks you a question in Mandarin and you want to reply in the negative, there is no word for a simple "no." You are forced to use the verb they used in their question, and then append the right negative prefix to it.

Similarly for "yes." The word most often used as a kind of "yes" is the verb *shi*, which means "is." (There are no verbal tenses in Mandarin the way Westerners understand them; verbs are not declined and there are no infinitives. Furthermore, there are no plurals in the usual sense: you don't add an "s" to the end of a noun to make it plural. All of this tends to make Mandarin a relatively imprecise language, more poetry than prose, in the eyes of some observers.) However, *shi* is not always the right word to use for an affirmation. If someone asks you if you want that sautéed scorpion, and you do, you reply in the affirmative using the verb they used. Thus, the correct answer to "Do you want the scorpion?" is *yao*. The correct positive response to "Do you have the contract?" is *you*. The correct negative response to a question that uses *shi*—such as "Are you an American?" (*ni shi mei guo ren ma?*) if you are, actually, a Canadian—would be *bu shi*. Literally "not is." The problem with *bu shi* for English-speaking people is that it sounds suspiciously like "bull-shit." When English speakers say "bullshit" it sounds like *bu shi* to the Chinese. Either way, though, the point gets across!

This lack of "yes" and "no" in the language provides room for some level of ambiguity we do not enjoy in the West. It also means that such absolutes as "yes" and "no" are anathema to the Chinese way of handling a business negotiation where everything must be subtle, misdirected, or simply "understood." You should never use the word "no" at any time during a negotiation: it is rude, and is considered to represent a total lack of flexibility and finesse. When asked if you can do something that you know is completely impossible, simply respond with "I will investigate the possibility. Allow me to confer with the colleagues back home," or something like that. Always leave the door open.

Numbers

I put numbers first because, well, that is what we really need to know right away. Most books on conversational Mandarin begin with "How are you?" and "Why is that shrimp still moving?" We, on the other hand, need to be able to communicate in numbers because that is what we do. Here then are the numbers, their *pinyin*-style pronunciations, and my own suggestion for pronunciation:

1	yi	ee	6	liu	lay-oh
2	er	are	7	qi	chee
3	san	san	8	ba	ba
4	si	sir	9	jiu	jee-oh
5	wu	wu	10	shi	shir

Although I have written the pronunciation for 6 and 9 as two syllables each, they are single syllables, so pronounce them as one.

To make numbers greater than ten, the Chinese combine the word for "ten" with the other appropriate digit. Thus, "eleven" becomes *shi yi* or *shir ee*.

11	shi yi	shir ee	16	shi liu	shir lay-oh

12	shi er	shir are	17	shi qi	shir chee
13	shi san	shir san	18	shi ba	shir ba
14	shi si	shir sir	19	shi jiu	shir jee-oh
15	shi wu	shir wu	20	er shi	are shir

Fooled you on that last one, right? When we get to the numbers above nineteen, the system changes. You will notice that "12" is pronounced *shi er* but that "20" is the reverse of that, *er shi,* which means, obviously, "two tens." Thus, "30" is "three tens" or *san shi,* etc. The phrase for "21" is therefore *er shi yi* or "two tens one."

21	er shi yi	are shir ee	26	er shi liu	are shir lay-oh
22	er shi er	are shir are	27	er shi qi	are shir chee
23	er shi san	are shir san	28	er shi ba	are shir ba
24	er shi si	are shir sir	29	er shi jiu	are shir jee-oh
25	er shi wu	are shir wu	30	san shi	san shir

The word for "100" is *yi bai,* which literally means "one hundred." Thus:

100	yi bai	ee buy	600	liu bai	lay-oh buy
200	er bai	are buy	700	qi bai	chee buy
300	san bai	san buy	800	ba bai	ba buy
400	si bai	sir buy	900	jiu bai	jee-oh buy
500	wu bai	wu buy	1000	yi qian	ee chee-en

Thus, the number "246" is rendered as *er bai si shi liu* or literally "two hundred four ten six." "555" (a brand of cigarette popular in China) is *wu bai wu shi wu* or "five hundred five ten five."

With the number for "thousand"—*qian*—we follow the same format:

1,000	yi qian	ee chee-en	6,000	liu qian	lay-oh chee-en
2,000	er qian	are chee-en	7,000	qi qian	chee chee-en
3,000	san qian	san chee-en	8,000	ba qian	ba chee-en
4,000	si qian sir	chee-en	9,000	jiu qian	jay-oh chee-en
5,000	wu qian	wu chee-en	10,000	yi wan	ee wahn

Oops. Why isn't "10,000" simply *shi qian?* Because it's not. The Chinese method of counting includes this anomaly, a separate designation for "ten thousand." The unit 10,000 is used from here on out, so that "100,000" becomes *shi wan* or "ten ten thousand" and "1,000,000" becomes *yi bai wan* or "one hundred ten thousand." You have to commit this method to memory because it will come in handy later when you are trying to communicate through your interpreter the cost for a gross of your widgets. Oh, by the way, there is a separate unit quantifier for "100,000,000" which is *yi yi* or "ee ee," which pretty much sums up my feelings on that as well.

The ordinal numbers are also useful, especially when your customers are enumerating the outstanding issues with your proposal. I have watched countless times as the spokesperson for the factory lists all the ways they don't love me: "First (*diyi*), your price is too high; second (*di er*), your quality is not as high as your competitor; third (*di san*), your price is still too high; fourth (*di si*), quality is negotiable."

For the sake of the exhausted entrepreneur who has just spent twenty-five hours getting to Beijing, in economy, and is jet-lagged and in no mood for levity, I enumerate the ordinals below:

First	di yi	dee ee	Sixth	di liu	dee lay-oh
Second	di er	dee are	Seventh	di qi	dee chee
Third	di san	dee san	Eighth	di ba	dee ba
Fourth	di si	dee sir	Ninth	di jiu	dee jee-oh
Fifth	di wu	dee wu	Tenth	di shi	dee shir

The alert reader will note that the creation of ordinals requires only the prefix *di* before the usual numbers. You can continue this until *di yi yi* or the one hundred millionth if you like.

Now you may have to deal with fractions, dozens, and that sort of thing in your negotiations. The following are representative samples of these.

1/2	er fen	zhi yi (or, more commonly: yi ban)
2/3	san fen	zhi er
3/4	si fen	zhi san
4/5	wu fen	zhi si

You will see that when the Chinese speak in fractions, they reverse the order Westerners would normally use, so that "two thirds" becomes "three fraction two." The word *fen* means literally "fraction"; the word *zhi* means . . . well, it's a little vague.

Decimals are a lot easier. You use the same numbers we began with, and simply "say" the decimal point. In other words:

The decimal number 1.45 becomes *yi dian si wu* or "one point four five." The word *dian* is the word for "point," so you insert that where you need it.

The word for "dozen" is *da*. One dozen is *yi da*, and so on. A half-dozen would be *ban da*. The word *ban* is the word for "half," such that *yi ban* means "one half."

There is one more anomaly of which you should be aware, and that is the word for "two." Above, you have already seen that the word for "two" is *er*. However, that is good only for counting. If someone asks you how many fingers he's holding up, though, you wouldn't use the word *er*. Instead, you would say *liang*, as in *liang ge* or "two things" (the word *ge* being a kind of all-around measure word; Mandarin is full of measure words, but *ge* will suffice for most things, even if it is not always grammatical). At a restaurant, a maitre d' may ask you "How many are in your party?" and (as long as he is not referring to the Communist Party) you might reply *Liang ge ren* or "two persons" or *liang wei*, which means pretty much the same thing. Don't ask me why *liang* and not *er*. It's just a fact of life.

Another number—without which Western civilization would never have achieved its greatness—is the cipher. Nought. Zero. Very useful if your room number happens to be 1007, as was mine in the Beijing Hotel so many times we thought it was certain that the room was bugged especially for foreign guests. Anyway, the word for "zero" is *ling,* so that the number 1007 would be pronounced *yi ling ling qi* when asking for your room key.

Polite Conversation

Having covered numbers as much as we want to, we now come to the niceties of Mandarin-language greetings and other polite forms of conversation. (The impolite forms will be covered below. They are also necessary, at least so that you know precisely how you are being insulted.)

The very first phrase anyone studying Mandarin always learns is:

Ni hao!

Pronounced "knee how" it means, simply, "you well!" It is an abbreviated form of the more precise *Ni hao ma?* or "Are you well?" It is a very useful distinction, for it has given us that great contribution of Mandarin to the philosophy of language and linguistics: the spoken question mark.

The word *ma* at the end of any sentence turns that sentence into a question. Because Mandarin is tonally inflected, Chinese people cannot speak a sentence and make it a question the way we do. In other words, we are able to say "You're sure you're eighteen?" with a rising tone at the end of the word "eighteen" that makes it a question when we say it. Otherwise, what we are saying is "You're sure you're eighteen," which is a statement and not a question, even though the words are exactly the same. Mandarin speakers do not have this luxury, because every syllable they speak has its own tone. Thus, they add the word *ma* at the end of the sentence just the way we use a rising tone at the end of a statement to turn it into a question. This way *Ni hao*—a statement— becomes *Ni hao ma?* a question.

A very popular greeting in Beijing when I was there in the 1980s was *Ni chi fan le ma?* which means "Have you eaten yet?" The appropriate response was *Chi bao le,* which roughly translated means "Ate my fill." It was the kind of self-congratulating exchange that was common in the years after the Great Leap Forward among those who had survived starvation.

So, a few common phrases:

Ni hao!	knee-how	Hello!
Ni hao ma?	knee-how ma?	How are you?
Wo hao, xie xie.	Wo how, shyeh shyeh	I'm fine, thank you.
Hen hao, xie xie.	hun hao, shyeh shyeh	Very fine, thank you.
Ni men hao!	knee mun how	How are you? (plural form)
Wo men hao, xie xie.	wo mun how, shyeh shyeh	We're fine, thank you.
Ni chi fan le ma?	knee chir fan luh ma?	Have you eaten yet?
Chi bao le, xie xie.	chir bao luh, shyeh shyeh	Ate my fill, thank you.
Xie xie ni.	sheh-shyeh knee.	Thank you.
Bu ke chi.	boo ker chee.	You're welcome.

Note: The Knights Who Say *Nin* (with a nod to Monty Python)

If you want to demonstrate that you are really polite, very respectful, and knowledgeable about the language, you can use *nin* instead of *ni*. *Nin* also means "you" but it is equivalent to *vous* in French or *usted* in Spanish, a more polite form usually used with people you don't know well or with those superior in rank to yourself. It would not be expected of a foreigner to be conscious enough of the differences to employ this term, so if the use of it is too confusing you can rest assured that *ni* will be entirely acceptable.

Qing wen	ching when	Excuse me (when you're trying to get someone's attention)
Dui bu qi	dway bu chee	Pardon me (when you've done or said something wrong)
Ni zao!	knee zow	Good morning!
Wan shang hao!	wahn shang hao	Good evening!
Wan an!	wahn Ahn	Good night!
Zai jian!	zie jee-ehn	Goodbye! (literally: until we meet again)
Ming tian jian!	ming tee-ehn jee-ehn	Until tomorrow!

And the most useful phrase in this book: *Wo bu hui jiang zhong guo hua*. I don't speak Chinese. Pronounced: *whoa boo hway jee-ang zhoong gwo huah*.

Business Terminology

I will give a quick glossary of common business terms. They will be useful to know, and when you get used to hearing Mandarin you will be able to pick them out of a conversation and have some idea what is being discussed.

Business	sheng yi, also mai mai	sheng yee, my my
Trade	mao yi	mow yee
Foreign trade	dui wai mao yi	dway why mow yee
International	guo ji	gwoh jee
Joint venture	he zi jing ying	huh ze jing ying
Negotiate	shang qia	shang chee-ah
Manufacture	zhi zao	zhir zow
Machine	ji qi	jee chee
Spare parts	bei jian	bay jee-ehn
Specifications	gui ge	gway guh
Product	chan pin	chan peen
Commodity	shang pin	shang peen
Catalog	mu lu	moo loo
Quote	bao	bow
Quantity	shu liang	shoe liang
Cost	hao fei	how fay
Price	jia ge	jee-ah guh
Market price	shi jia	shir jee-ah
Unit price	dan jia	dan jee-ah
Firm offer	shi pan	shir pan
Sell	xiao, or xiao shou	shee-ow, shee-ow show
Buy	mai jin	my jeen
Order	ding, or ding gou	ding, ding go
Place an order	ding huo	ding hwoh
Supply	gong huo	gong hwoh
Discount	zhe kou	zher koh
Freight	yun fei	yoon fay
Insurance	bao xian fei	bow shee-an fay

FOB	chuan shang jiao huo jia	chuan shang jee-ow hwoh jee-ah
CIF	dao an jia	dow an jee-ah
Time of delivery	jiao huo qi	jee-ow hwoh chee
Director	jing li	jing lee
Managing Director	zong jing li	zong jing lee
Vice-Managing Director	fu zong jing li	foo zong jing lee
Agent	dai li shang	die li shang
Salesman	tui xiao yuan	tway shee-ow yu-en
Bank	yin hang	een hang
US dollar	mei yuan	may yu-en
British pound	ying bang	eeng banh
Japanese yen	ri yuan	ruh yu-en
Hong Kong dollar	gang yuan	gong yu-en
Contract	he tong	huh tong
Letter of credit	xin yong zheng	sheen yong zheng
Documents	dan ju	dan joo
Finance	jin rong	jeen rong
Pay	zhi fu	zhir foo
Guarantee	dan bao	dan bow
Sales confirmation	xiao shou que ren shu	shee-ow show tsweh ren shoe
Letter of guarantee	bao zheng han	bow zheng han
Expense	fei yong	fay yong
Buyer	mai fang	my fung
Customer	ke hu, or gu ke	kuh who, or goo kuh
End-user	yong hu	yong who
Brand	pai hao	pie how

To Get Drunk Is Glorious

Another very important business term is *gan bei!* or "empty glass," the most common toast in Mandarin and one you will hear a lot of during banquets, lunches, karaoke sessions, every day, everywhere. You are expected to literally empty your glass when you hear this toast. The correct method is to drain it, then show that it is truly empty by holding it upside down. You can sometimes squirm out of this by saying *yi ban*, or "one half." But then you have to drink exactly half, no less. You can't use this tactic during the first round of toasts, however, or you will be perceived as unfriendly at worst or a total wuss at best. Save it for later on in the evening when you're certain you won't be able to make it home without passing out. Remember that toasts are given with everything from beer—*pi jiu*—to *mao tai*. A tall glass of beer has to emptied just as if it were a tiny liqueur glass. Good luck.

Impolite Conversation

As promised, herewith some terms and phrases that you may never hear directed at you or your general direction, but of which you should nonetheless be aware. Please refrain from using them yourself. You could get into a lot of trouble if you do.

Bullshit!	Fang pi!	Fahng pee
Damn it!	Gai ze!	Guy zeh
Fuck you!	Ta ma da!	Ta ma da
Foreign devil	guei ze or yang guei ze	gway zeh, or yang gway ze
Foreigner	wai guo ren (a more polite form!) why gwoh ren	
	lao wai (also polite, meaning "old foreigner") laow why	

You can always rely on *xiao xin* (shee-ow sheen) which means "careful!" (literally translated: little heart).

A good way to end this appendix, and this book.

Xiao xin!

Acknowledgments

This book is the product of more than thirty years in international business, most of that time spent in China, so the list of persons to acknowledge and thank is too long to give in its entirety here. All I can do is highlight some of the people who helped form my understanding and capability in China trade, and hope that all the others will forgive me for not mentioning their names.

First of all, thanks must go to Anthony Chang—Zhang An De—for bringing me to China in the first place. We had a hell of a ride, and there was no better traveling companion. His generosity of spirit was remarkable; his sense of humor made the four years we spent wheeling and dealing, wining and dining, and moving and shaking all the more bearable and enjoyable. I should also like to mention Anthony's brother, Zhang Li De, as well as Anthony's niece, Zhang Qiang, who helped make China manageable, entertaining, and instructive, smoothing out the wrinkles from time to time and making everything "flat."

Secondly, Peter Wong deserves special mention. A patient, wise, hardworking and accomplished businessman who can easily bridge the gap between East and West with his intimidating business background in China, Europe, and North America, Peter Wong brought a positive attitude and multitasking competence to the table.

Together, we covered thousands upon thousands of miles in China, held dozens of seminars, hundreds of business negotiations, and signed millions of dollars worth of contracts . . . even if that meant drinking copious amounts of Carlsberg, much to my patently hypocritical dismay.

Wang Lei, Peter's talented and beautiful spouse, also deserves mention, not only for her patience in dealing with his constant traveling and late-night strategizing but for her contribution to the advertising and marketing elements of our China trade.

In Malaysia, where I was located for seven of those years spent in China business, I have to thank Cecelia Ang Ai Kheng, whose consistent contribution to the organizing and running of my offices in several countries at once meant that I could concentrate on the sales aspects of the business secure in the knowledge that every other aspect—including many of the marketing issues, but also the day-to-day human resources, bookkeeping, and accounting nightmares—were being taken care of in Cecelia's inimitably professional fashion. Fluent in three languages, she is frighteningly efficient and good-natured at the same time. As a businesswoman, she has been—and remains—a highly valuable resource.

In Singapore, Tham Yar Leong was my connection to the world of kiasu businesspeople. Running two of my offices in Singapore—first for one company, then another— Tham's insider knowledge of the industry, the people, and the culture helped make us famous and brought considerable credibility to our corporate profile. His knowledge of *feng shui* helped in other aspects, as well!

I would also like to thank a number of other people, including those at the Industrial and Commercial Bank of China, China Telecom, the Beijing Telephone Company, all the wonderful people in the city of Baoding, our friends in Qingdao, Shanghai, Hong Kong, Chengdu, Chongqing, Urumuqi, Hohhot, Nanjing . . . the list is endless. Thanks also to those American and European business executives who took a chance on me and on China, including General Electric (the Erie, Pennsylvania plant);

the former Digital Equipment Corporation; Hi-Tech Extrusion Systems; Ortronics; Cooper Tire and Rubber; Superior Modular Products; Ericsson Cables of Sweden; Ruemmer Maschinenbau of Bamberg, Germany; to Ken Brownell, for a memorable visit in Rome and for taking a chance in China; to my good friend Gennaro Oliva, for his professionalism and generosity over the years; and to the late Steve Orlando, who celebrated our success with champagne one winter's day in Mystic, Connecticut.

To the staff at Continuum and to my long-suffering editor, Frank Oveis, many thanks for your enthusiasm and support for this project, which was contagious!

Lastly, to the faculty at Florida International University and most especially to Dr. Steven Heine, whose class on Asian Values in Business inspired this work.

My sincere thanks to all of you.

Bibliographic Note

The quotations that appear in this volume are all taken from published writings and speeches of Chairman Mao Ze Dong ranging from his early days as a guerrilla fighter in China in the 1920s, to the "Great Imperialist War" period of the 1930s and 1940s and then to the Cultural Revolution period of the 1960s.

The greatest source of quotations comes from the Little Red Book—as it was popularly known—or The Quotations of Chairman Mao TseTung as it was formally entitled. My copy dates from 1967 and was published by the Foreign Languages Press of Beijing.

Other valuable resources for Mao's writing and thought include:

The Selected Works of Chairman Mao, Foreign Languages Press, Beijing, in multiple volumes, published in 1977.

The Selected Writings of Mao Ze Dong, Foreign Languages Press, Beijing, 1945

The Writings of Mao Zedong, published by M.E Sharpe, 1986.

Another source is the Joint Publications Research Service of the US Government, which released in English translation The Collected Works of Mao Tse-Tung (1917-1949) in 1978, now freely available online as PDF files.

Index

DATE DUE